This Book Is for You, if You're...

- Buying a home
- Planning to refinance your high interest loan
- Evaluating home equity line of credit offers
- Tempted by a reverse mortgage
- Worried your current mortgage payments have been miscalculated
- Wanting your lender to stop assessing "PMI" and real estate tax impound charges
- Not thrilled about the prospect of sitting around financially naked, with a loan advisor whose financial knowhow can tie you and your pocketbook in knots for more than a quarter of a century.

This book gives you the weapons you need to go out and hunt down not only the best rates, but the best loan program specifics that match your needs.

Unlike many books on financing, you don't have to trudge through the whole thing from beginning to end before you start interviewing lenders. Each piece of information is short, as stand-alone as possible, and alphabetized so that you can locate it quickly.

Some Important tools you'll find in this book:

√ How to calculate your own borrower qualification ratios, so you'll know ahead of time how large a loan amount you can get.

√ The three most important questions you need to ask every lender you're considering.

√ Why principal paydowns offer better savings than 15 year amortization or bi-weekly payment mortgages.

√ Why recasting can turn a bad loan program into a true nightmare.

√ The most important thing to watch out for in a cash-out refinance.

√ How to use our Loan Evaluation Checklist to stack up the true costs of any loan program.

√ Know when you should tell your lender *"No."*

√ Where to find financing for co-ops, farms and other "non-standard" types of property.

√ What kinds of "clouds" on your title report can cause your property to lose value.

√ Two lender turnaround deadlines that can make or break your deal.

√ When to go ahead with a loan, even though the amount isn't what you need.

√ How to solve past credit problems with affordable, no nonsense counseling, and lenders willing to help you buy your house, now.

√ How to tap into MCC tax credits to get IRS help with your homebuying.

√ VA programs — no down and cheap. How to find lenders who have streamlined the process, can qualify you and fund quickly.

And lots and lots of GOODIES, including:
ALL NEW extensive Money$ource Directory to lenders, government programs, tax savings, nonprofit counselors and free software
COMPLETE "Apples to Apples" Loan Evaluators
SIMPLE Refinance Evaluator
TRIAL RUN Loan Qualifying Worksheet
EASY Loan Payment Estimator

STEINERS COMPLETE

HOW TO TALK MORTGAGE TALK

By Clyde and Shari Steiner

From the Authors of
Steiners Complete
How to Move Handbook

Design by
Lionel Storch

ïP.

Independent
Information
Publications
Consumers
Series
San Francisco, CA
94110

www.movedoc.com

Published by the IIP Consumer Series, an imprint of **Independent Information Publications**, San Francisco, CA 94110. For information on where to purchase this book, please call 1-800 444-2524 Extension 1. For information on bulk or premium sales, please call the Bulk Sales Desk at 415 643 8600.

First Printing May 1998
Second Printing September 1998
Revised Second Edition February 1999

Steiners Complete How-To-Move Handbook, **by the same authors, covers all aspects of relocating your home and family, and is also available at better bookstores or by direct order from 1-800 444-2524 ext 1.**

Library of Congress Cataloging in Publication Data
Library of Congress Catalog Card No: 99-60352
Steiner, Clyde L.
       Steiners complete how-to-talk mortgage talk.
       Includes glossary.
       Includes appendix.
       p.   cm.   10 9 8 7 6 5 4 3 2
       ISBN 0-913733-12-1
       1. Mortgage loans — United States.
       2. Real estate business — United States — finance.
       I. Steiner, Shari Y. II. Steiner, Clyde L. III. Title.

Printed in the United States of America
Published simultaneously in Canada

About the Authors

Clyde and Shari Steiner are nationally recognized relocation experts and longtime journalists. Their writings and seminars on "hunting and bagging the best loans" are the result of having obtained dozens of loans for themselves and Shari's real estate clients in the course of the last fifteen years. Their personal experience with mortgage markets spans times when money has been cheap and readily available and times when rates were in double digits.

They are the co-authors of *Steiners Complete How to Move Handbook*, and Clyde writes a monthly column on technology in real estate offices for *California Real Estate* magazine.

Shari writes on various relocation topics for major national women's magazines. She is a practicing California Realtor, who manages her own small office. In the past she has developed the training materials for loan officers of a major national Lender.

They oversee Independent Information Publications' annual *Independent Relocation Survey* conducted at www.move-doc.com.

They find mortgage questions and complaints about the mortgage process make up one of the largest section of their "Ask the Moving Doctors" online column.

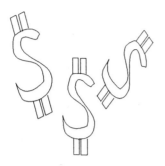

Steiners Complete

HOW TO TALK MORTGAGE TALK

Table of Contents

Appendix

Mortgage Quest: The Hunter at Work

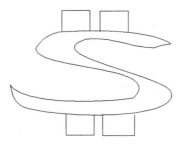

Financial pundits often intone that your home will be your single largest purchase in your lifetime. This is not true. Hidden behind all the discussions about the complexities of buying a home is a little known fact:

Your mortgage interest paid over the next 30 years will cost you, at a 7.5% interest **Rate,** *one-and-a-half times* the purchase price of your home. If **Rates** bounce up to 12% or worse, as they did for extended periods in the 80's, the interest you're paying will run you *nearly three times* the purchase price of your home!

Whoa there! This mortgage hunt stuff means serious money! Although readers may quickly point out that we haven't taken into account the influence of inflation and the future value of money, we haven't taken into account the way an **Amortization Schedule** weighs time in favor of the lender, either.

At 12%, a $100,000 loan wracks up $62,000 in payments over the first five years. The lender receives $59,000+ of that as interest. And that's before we add in the upfront **Closing Costs.**

Not only is this serious money for you as an individual, mortgage lending is big business. Home mortgage debt in the U.S. currently stands at slightly more than a trillion dollars. Essentially, you're girding yourself up to go hunting in one of the biggest public money markets in the world.

It may be axiomatic, but it's wise to remember as you embark—lenders are in the money business because they like selling money. They spend their time and energy figuring out **Loan Programs** the way Detroit works away on aerodynamics. They delight in bringing out new models every year with fancy trim and a blinding selection of new colors and new names, to entice new homebuyers and seduce the **Refi-**inclined.

Since **Adjustable Loans** were introduced two decades ago, your monthly payment has been only one of several variables that can make the difference between your best deal and your worst nightmare. It's no fluke that the fancier the **Loan Program,** in terms of **Teaser Rates** and high **Loan to Value,** the more it's going to cost you later.

Besides the complex array of **Loan Program** choices, there are numerous myths that obscure the most effective ways to hunt:

Myth #1—Negotiating the Hunt

Myth: You can negotiate a better loan.

Truth: In today's lending industry, you can only negotiate loans in the rare case where you find a **Seller Carryback** for the **First,** or you find one of the few remaining **Portfolio** lenders who can tailor their **Loan Programs.**

Ninety-five percent of the loans that are available are offered by huge, national lending institutions catering to the **Secondary Market.** A skilled **Loan Advisor** will help you find the **Loan Program** that best fits your needs, but he or she can no more change significant **Terms** of that loan than a car salesman can redesign a car.

To give you the illusion of negotiation, many lenders currently allow you to lower your **Rate** by paying more in upfront **Fees.** Your **Loan Advisor** should also suggest numerous ways to help you **Qualify** for a higher **Loan Amount,** if you want.

You have to oversee this process carefully, but the primary skill you need to hone is hunting, not negotiating. Once you've worked out what kind of loan you want, you need to hunt down the best **Loan Advisor** and **Loan Program.**

Bagging the best loan for your home **Purchase** or **Refinance** can save you many thousands of dollars. This book will arm you with the weapons that you need.

Myth #2—Friends and Partners

Myth: The **Loan Advisor** is your friend.

Truth: Even if you've been buddies with this man or woman for years, the **Loan Advisor** always gets paid by the lender. And, 99% of the time, he or she is paid by commission.

He or she won't get paid, however, if you don't find the loan you want. The **Loan Advisor** therefore becomes a hunting partner. Unfortunately, this partner is tethered to his or her company. If that company doesn't offer the loan you need (and even the biggest **Mortgage Brokers** don't work with all **Loan Programs**), he or she has to convince you to change your goals...or you have to get a new hunting partner.

Don't misunderstand us. The **Loan Advisor** is crucial to your hunt. Good ones are like good stock brokers. They not only help you ferret out good **Loan Programs,** their services are timesaving and provide help every step of the way. **Loan Advisors** like helping you—but they still always get paid by the lender.

Myth #3—Purchases

Myth: The sequence of events is:
1. Find a house.
2. Negotiate the price.
3. Find a loan.

Truth: The reverse—decide on a loan with a monthly payment that works for your budget, then go looking for a home in the price range that matches your financing.

Going at it this way saves time, particularly when you get the lender to give you a **Pre-Approval Commitment**. The strategy not only gives you peace of mind, it provides a good negotiating tool with a seller, because your offer includes the ability to close quickly.

*Tip: Get a lender to **Pre-Approve** you, not just give you a **Pre-Qualification**. Have them review your written **Application** and give you the approximate amount they'll finance in writing.*

*Don't settle for just a quick telephone **Pre-Qualification**. You don't want unexpected problems coming up when you go back to the lender ready to take out your loan.*

*Trap: Regardless of a written **Pre-Approval**, you still must make your **Purchase** offer contingent upon getting your mortgage. Otherwise, rising interest **Rates**, a low **Appraisal** or an unethical lender can leave you without your loan... And a seller who can sue you for breach of contract.*

Myth #4—Refinances

Myth: Timing a **Refi** is up to you.

Truth: We're great believers in the concept (not exactly a myth) that a **Refinance** should offer the blessings of time and focus.

Alas, the truth for us has been that nine times out of ten, we've been **Refinancing** under the gun of a **Second Mort-**

gage coming due, the need for cash for some other reason, or—our most stressful loanhunt experience—an **Interest Rate** market that's started moving up.

Try to do as we say do, not as we've done. Note the past tense—we're hoping to better our practices, too.

If you've gone into your existing loan knowing you'll want to **Refi** within several years for whatever reason, keep an eye on the **Rate Sheets** that appear regularly in newspaper real estate sections or on the Internet.

See **Rate Watch Services** in the **National Money$ource Directory** in the **Appendix**.

Tip: If you've got a deadline for a **Refi**, start the loanhunt a good 18 months ahead of time. If **Rates** start going down, start serious interviewing. Most loans don't have a **Prepayment Penalty**, but you're looking at big problems if you don't complete your **Refi** by your deadline.

Trap: Lenders hate being caught with a **Rate Lock** when **Rates** start going up again significantly. If your **Application** is being processed at such a time, look out for the lender's **Qualifications** getting stiffer and/or the **Appraisal** coming in too low to give you the **Loan Amount** you need. This is another time when you need to have at least a **Double App**, so you can try to make the loan elsewhere. Unfortunately, our experience has been that all lenders are reluctant to provide **Funding** when the market is moving up.

Tip: If you're fairly certain the **Rate** market's bottomed, and there's any way you can meet the revised lender **Ratios** or **Appraisal**, we recommend going for it. That's how we got a 5.75% **30-Year Fixed** in the mid-90's. Of course, coming up with an additional $20,000 for the **Closing** wasn't pleasant.

Myth #5—Home Equity, Reverse Mortgages, etc.

Myth: These loans will save you money.

Truth: Despite the friendly tone and the informal language of the offers that clog your mailbox, both real and virtual, most are as nefarious as the credit card "checks" that offer such wonderful ease of use...and humongous cash advance charges plus the highest rate the company issues.

There are a few good, alternative **Loan Programs** out there, however. Finding and evaluating them is one of the important missions of this book.

Seven Steps
to Savvy
Loan hunting

1. Your first step is knowing the terrain—you must understand the language and scope out current market possibilities. Read through the following **Glossary** to get up to speed on industry jargon and get comfortable with the **Loan Evaluation Checklist** and **Loan Amount Qualifying Worksheets** that follow in the **Appendix.** Use the **Credit Report Request** sample letter in the **Appendix** to get a copy of your report, and review.

2. Ask your real estate agent, your **Title Company,** your **Lawyer,** and your friends and relatives for lender recommendations.

Check the **National Money$ource Directory,** browse the Internet and clip local newspaper real estate sections for lender ads and **Rate** lists. Select five to ten lenders and/or **Mortgage Brokers** that seem to have a **Loan Program** you want, and fill in our **Loan Evaluation Checklists** with their telephone numbers and/or Internet addresses.

3. Start contacting them and filling in the rest of the **Loan Evaluation Checklists.** Most lenders will offer more than one **Loan Program,** with different **Rates, Fees,** and **Terms.**

On initial calls, tell the lender your **Property Type** (i.e., single family, condo, or co-op, 2-4 family), the city it's located in, the **Loan Amount** you're looking for, and whether you're looking for an **Adjustable** or a **Fixed Loan.** They will tell you if they can make the kind of loan you need.

4. Stop answering questions and start asking. Find out who you're speaking with and the **Program Name** of the loan being recommended.

5. Go for the "Basic Three" on the **Loan Evaluation Checklist,** i.e., "What are your **Rates, Total Upfront Lender Fees,** and **Turnaround Times?**" Ask them to send you their **Rate Sheets,** which will often answer all your questions much faster than interviewing.

Many lenders have **Rate Sheets** on their Internet sites. Others won't even mail a flyer, saying **Rates** will be changed by the time you get them.

Although this is common, be particularly careful with lenders who won't explain their **Loan Programs** in writing. We've seen them vary loan costs more than 250% over their original verbal promise.

6. When you've weeded out which three or four **Loan Programs** seem best, go back and talk with those **Loan Advisors** again. This time, review and fill in any blanks on the **Loan Evaluation Checklist** (see the **Appendix**), including actual dollar amounts for **Fees** and **Maximum Payments** from year to year.

Treat this interview like a doctor's visit. Expect to be financially undressed, and to both ask and answer financial questions you wouldn't discuss with your mother. Ask for an **Application** package, so you can fill it in later at your leisure.

7. Stack up your choices, select the loan you want and start filling in the **Application.** Keep asking the **Loan Advisor** questions about anything that you don't understand or that seems unreasonably expensive or risky. If you're dealing with a lender you haven't been able to check out locally, you may want to consider doing a **Double App**—applying to two lenders at once.

You're better off paying two **Application** and **Appraiser Fees,** and going with the best **Loan Program** a lender will commit to in writing, than getting stuck at closing with large unexpected **Fees,** or a lowered **Loan Amount,** or, worst of all, a lender who suddenly won't do your loan at all.

Envision the months stretching ahead with payments several hundreds of dollars lower than you'd be paying with most of the **Loan Programs** out there.

Keep asking savvy questions and re-evaluating the possibilities. You'll be glad you did.

Glossary of Mortgage Terms and Strategies

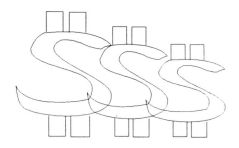

NOTE: The following terms are in alphabetical order for ease of use when you come across a word or concept you don't know. If this is the first time you've gotten a loan or you haven't talked to a lender for several years, it's a good idea to browse the list for an overview before starting your interviews.

All words in bold are cross-referenced in this list, so if the definition of one term isn't enough, you can check the other terms involved.

15-Year / 30-Year / 40-Year Fixed—Mortgages are often identified by their **Term,** i.e., the length of time it takes to pay them off. This is particularly true with **Fixed Rate Loans.** The most common **Term** is the **30-Year,** but lenders are currently offering both longer and shorter **Terms.**

The **15-Year** loan usually has a lower **Rate** and/or a lower **Origination Fee** than the **30-Year Fixed,** but has larger monthly payments because you're paying off more of the **Principal** each month. The **Loan Payment** chart in the **Appendix** shows you how much the amounts differ.

Advantages—You're building **Equity** faster and you're paying less **Interest** than you would with a **30-Year Fixed.**

Disadvantages—The **Equity** you're building with the bank is not liquid so it's hard to reinvest. If you need to pull your cash **Equity** out by getting a **Second** or **Refinancing,** you may have to take a loan at a higher **Rate. Purchase Loans** are always at the cheapest **Rate** you can find. A lower monthly payment for a **30-Year Fixed** loan leaves cash for investing or buying other things.

The **40-Year** has an even lower monthly, due to repayment's being stretched out over a longer period.

See also **Amortization** and **Fixed.**

"A," "B," "C," "D" Credit Rating—An **"A"** credit loan applicant has borrowed in the past and shown a consistent pattern of responsible (i.e., on time) repayment. If you've been late on payments, even a $29 credit card bill, you can have a **Ding On Your Credit.** If you've been late more than twice, it's considered a major **Ding,** and you'll have some explaining to do to meet many lender's **Borrower Qualifications.**

The more **Dings,** the lower your rating, the worst being a **"D"**—when you've been through a bankruptcy and/or fore-closure during the last seven years. If you find you're in the **"B"** or **"C"** rating, try the higher **Rate** lenders that advertise on the Internet and in large newspapers. If you're a **"D,"** set up a repayment plan with any remaining outstanding debts, establish a regular payment history, and expect that most lenders will be reluctant to talk home loans with you until at least three years after either a bankruptcy or foreclosure.

Lenders are currently experimenting with fine tuning these **Credit Ratings** to **"A-," "B+,"** etc., so that they can further adjust their **Rates** when making loans.

See also **Credit Report, Credit Rating,** and **FICO Rating.**

Adjustable Loan / Mortgage—Other common names include an **"ARM (Adjustable Rate Mortgage)"** or a "Variable Loan." Your monthly loan payments fluctuate according to an underlying **Index**. There are many varieties, but only two major types—those with and those without **Negative Amortization**. If there is no **Negative Amortization**, the loan is often called a **No Neg Loan**.

Lenders prefer **Adjustables** to **Fixed** because the borrower bears a major part of the risk of rising **Rates**. To promote them, they offer lower **Initial Rates**, higher **Loan Amounts**, and lower **Origination Fees**. When money is tight, many banks only offer **Adjustables**.

However, because your **Adjustable** payment changes can wreck your budget, you need to be particularly careful about signing on for this type of loan. Be sure your **Loan Advisor** writes out a **Maximum Payment Scenario**, so you have a complete idea of the risk you're taking.

*Tip: Lenders with **Adjustable Loans** will often allow somewhat higher **Ratios**. This means that if you're willing to spend as much as 40% of your income on your reoccurring expenses, and your credit is good, the lender might qualify you for a larger **Loan Amount**.*

*Tip: We advise considering an **Adjustable** only when you plan to leave or **Refinance** within three to five years or you need it in order to **Qualify** for the **Loan Amount** you want. An **Adjustable** should start off at least 4% cheaper than a **Fixed** (including all **Loan Fees**). It absolutely should not have **Negative Amortization**. Stick to your schedule of leaving or **Refinancing** within a maximum of five years. By that time your **Rate** will almost certainly be on par or even higher than a market **Fixed Rate Loan**.*

Affiliated Companies—Companies offering services connected with your obtaining your loan, which are owned by or otherwise **Affiliated** to your lender. The lender is required to **Disclose** possible **Affiliations** with their **Truth in Lending** documents when you make out your loan **Application**.

Trap: Some services, like **Appraisal**, **Tax Notification**, *or* **Flood Certification**, *can be automatically charged with your* **Closing Costs**. *Others, like* **Hazard** *or* **Flood Insurance**, *can only be charged if you fail to provide your own policy.*

 Tip: Always ask what services you can obtain separately, and shop several providers for those services. You can almost always save money with an outside provider.

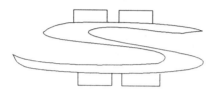

Amortization—The process by which the **Principal Loan Amount** you borrowed "dies off" a little with each month's payment until the entire amount is paid off—most commonly after 30 years. The **Principal** portion of your monthly payment is small in the first years, with most of the payment going to **Interest**. Later, the **Principal Amortization** dollars slowly become a larger part of the payment, even though, with a **Fixed**, the actual payment amount remains the same. The result is that in later years you have less tax deductible interest, but more of your payment is going to **Amortize**—pay off—the loan.

Amortization Schedule—The columns of numbers that tell you and the lender how much of your payment each month is allocated to **Interest** and how much to **Principal**. There are many **Online Amortization Schedule** programs listed in our **National Money$ource Directory**. The best ones include "cumulative cost" columns, which tell you the total amount you will have spent over time.

*Tip: On our **Loan Amount Qualifying Worksheet**, we ask you to total up your expenses for the first five years as you're evaluating which loan is best for you. You may want to modify this question to three years—if you're planning on moving soon—or longer than five years, if that's your intent.*

Annual Percentage Rate—See **APR.**

Application—Usually refers to the lengthy **Uniform Residential Loan Application (URLA)** questionnaire that nearly all lenders currently require a borrower to fill out as the first step in applying for the loan. It used to be that there were as many different **Application** forms as lenders, but with the strength of the **Secondary Market,** which requires a **URLA,** even **Portfolio** lenders have gone to the standard form.

See also **CLO** and **Online Application.**

*Tip: Get a URLA form from a **Loan Advisor** (or On-line) and fill it out very early in the loanhunting process, so that you know you've assembled all the required information. You should always work from the same original draft form if you decide to **Double App** more than one lender.*

*Tip: Always keep your own copy of the **Application** that you've given a lender. You'll need to refer to it as questions come up during the **Underwriting/Processing** stage, and even after you've been granted the loan, it's wise to keep the **Application** along with the other **Loan Agreement** papers you'll receive, If you ever have a disagreement with a lender as to how the loan is to be administered, you'll need to know everything said on all signed documents.*

Application Fee—Lenders don't like you to apply to more than one institution at a time. When money is tight and it's hard to get a loan, they often insist on an **Application Fee,** which is forfeit if you don't take their loan. This **Fee** usually runs between $100 and $200. Almost always the **Fee** is fully refundable if they don't grant you the loan they've offered you, although sometimes they insist on keeping the portion they've already spent on the **Credit Check** and the **Appraisal.** The amount and policy differs widely from bank to bank, so always include questions about their **Application Fee** in your **Loan Evaluation.**

Appraisal—The written assessment of the **Market Value** of the home. The appraiser usually works full time for the lender, but can be an outside consultant.

In either case, you typically pay an **Appraisal Fee** as a borrower **Closing Cost,** but you don't always automatically get a copy of the **Appraisal**—apparently because there's a fear you'll use it to press for a revision. Ask for it. The law now *guarantees* you can have it, if you pay for it, but the tradition of not giving it dies hard.

See also **Market Value.**

Tip: Don't be afraid to press for a revision if something seems wrong. Appraisers make mistakes, just like anybody else. We've seen appraisers reconsider which **Comparables** *to select or even admit they missed an entire section of the house being appraised.*

Appreciation—When the **Market Value** of your home goes up. Reasons for **Appreciation** include work you might do to improve your home's condition, changes in the neighborhood, or a rising economy.

APR (Annual Percentage Rate)—The **APR** formula takes the basic **Interest Rate** and adds in the lender's **Closing Costs.**

By law, all lenders must quote you their **APR** as well as their **Interest Rate. APR**—in concept—makes it easy to compare the costs of different loans. It does work fairly well when comparing different lender's **Fixed Mortgages.** Unfortunately, the **APR** formula is not sophisticated enough to reflect the wide variations possible with **Adjustable Loans,**

so today's comparisons need real **Maximum Payment** calculations.
See the **Loan Evaluation Checklist** in the **Appendix**.

Assumable—If **Interest Rates** are high in the lending market when you go to sell, your buyer may want to **Assume** the existing loan. Most **Adjustable Loans** are **Assumable,** if the buyer **Qualifies** and pays an **Assumption Fee.** Most **Fixed Loans** and **Seconds** are not **Assumable.**

Attorney—See **Lawyer.**

AUS (Automated Underwriting Service)—The big, **Secondary Market** financing pools now offer this service to **Mortgage Brokers** and lenders, who can do their paperwork on a mainframe computer directly hooked up to the Stock Market pools.

This means that **Underwriting** your loan for resale to the **Secondary Market** can be done far more quickly and effectively than the old, paper system, although it's not nearly as efficient or instantaneous as the credit card swipe machines you now encounter in the supermarket.

 *Trap: Despite the fact that this computerization cuts costs for the **Secondary Market** and the **Mortgage Broker** or lender **Underwriting** your loan, the Fee for this service (sometimes as much as $100+) is often passed on to you as one of your borrower **Closing Costs**.*

Bait and Switch—Sadly, we've known a number of **Loan Advisors** who apparently believe that lying about low **Rate Loan Program** availability will build their business. Recently, we even spent six weeks with a **Mortgage Broker** dangling a wonderful low **Rate Program** before us...who then **Switched** to a high **Rate**, 10% **Fee Program** at the last minute. Our surveys confirm that this tactic is common nationwide.

We're happy to report that we escaped from our lying person (we can hardly call her a **Loan Advisor**) by activating a **Double App** with another **Loan Advisor**, who'd been honest about her **Rates** and **Fees.**

*Tip: Although there are ways to complain to the Office of the Comptroller of Currency (see the **National Money$ource Directory** for information) about **Bait and Switch** tactics, they are hard to prove, and, as far as we know, impossible to use as a lever to force a lender into revising your **Loan Program**. This is the major reason we recommend a **Double App.***

Balloon Payment—Perhaps more appropriately, this is sometimes called a **"Bullet Loan."** This is a loan that has to be paid off before the **Principal** is **Fully Amortized.** Almost all **Seconds** have **Balloon Payments** at the end of five or seven years.

Some institutions offer lower **Rates** on **Fixed Rate Firsts** with a **Balloon Payment** coming due in five, seven, ten, or fifteen years, but the monthly loan payments calculated as though the loan **Amortization Term** was still 30 years.

These loans are often called "a 30 due in 10," etc. They may also carry a **Prepayment Penalty** for much of the life of the loan, so that there is only a period of six to twelve months during which you can pay off this loan and replace it with another.

*Tip: This loan is not for the faint of heart, but, because the **Rate** can be very competitive, we do recommend it if you know you'll be moving, or be able to Refinance, as the **Balloon Payment** comes due.*

*Ask if the lender has an "automatic **Rollover** proviso" to guarantee a **Refinance** for you when the **Balloon** comes due. They may refuse to put a guarantee into the mortgage contract itself, but still write you a letter stating that **Rollovers** have been their general policy.*

*Except in very tight markets, they will usually **Refi-**
nance—at the going market **Rate**—so long as you have
a clean payment history. Ask what the **Rollover Fee** is. It
should be less than your current **Origination Fee**, because they already know your good **Credit**. Unfortunately,
it's common for the lender to stipulate that the **Fee** will
be set at the time of the **Rollover**. If money is tight at
that time, the **Fee** can be higher.*

B/C Lenders—Also known as **Subprime Lenders.**
Lenders who specialize in mortgages for individuals with
"Less Than Perfect" **Credit Rating.** Does not actually stand
for "Bad Credit," but rather a score on the **Credit Rating.**
See also **"A," "B," "C," "D" Credit Rating.**

Beneficiary Statement—See **Payoff.**

Bi-Weekly Payment Mortgage—Some **Adjustables**
have the borrower make payments every two weeks instead
of once a month. The advantage to you is that paying **Principal** more often results in faster **Amortization,** thus saving
you significant **Interest** payments over the **Life** of the loan.
   See **Principal Paydown Payments** for a more flexible,
less stressful, **Interest** savings solution.

*Tip: We don't recommend this **Loan Program**, unless you are a very disciplined bill payer or you set this
schedule up as a direct deposit to your lender from your
regular checking account.*

Blanket Mortgage—A loan that covers more than one
property. Large commercial property owners often set up
Blanket Loans to cover a number of office buildings, shopping centers, and/or industrial parks, but such loans are rare
in home mortgage situations except for the basic loan on co-
op apartment buildings.
   An underlying co-op loan is secured by the land and the
co-op agreement between all the owners. If one of those
owners **Defaults** on his or her payments, it's up to the other
owners to make it up, as the lender can only foreclose against

the entire property, not the individual owner. Typically, a co-op buyer obtains a **Second Loan** against his or her individual unit. These loans can be hard to find, costly, and risky for the other owners.

Borrower Qualifications—Institutions require you to have enough cash to cover your **Downpayment** and **Closing Costs** plus an **"A" Credit Rating.** If you're self-employed, they may want a bank account large enough to cover several months of loan payments, in the event your business has some bad times.

At one time, lenders determined the amount of loan you **Qualified** for by simply multiplying your gross income times two or three, depending inversely on how high loan **Rates** were. However, gross income multipliers are rarely used anymore because today's consumers often have heavy payments for other debts. Instead, lenders require a set percentage **Ratio** of your income to cover your loan payment plus the rest of your long-term obligations.

To find out how your own **Ratios** work, photocopy several of the **Loan Amount Qualifying Worksheets** in the **Appendix** so that you can run the formulas a couple of different ways.

Use the sum of all household income as 100%. You can include investment or interest income, but you can't average in the profit you made from the sale or your last house or a killing made at the races. Lenders only want "ongoing income" i.e., income that's likely to continue over the next five years.

For most **Fixed Rate** loans, your payments for the loan **Principal, Interest, Real Estate Taxes,** and home **Insurance** (called the **"PITI"** monthly payment) can't exceed 28% of your income. Also, all your reoccurring expenses (your car loan, income tax, credit card payments, student loan, alimony, etc.) plus **PITI** can't exceed 36% of your total income. This means that if your non-**PITI** reoccurring expenses exceed 8% of your gross income, every dollar you spend there will dilute your loan-qualifying dollars.

Lenders have less stringent **Borrower Qualification Ratios** for many **Adjustable Loans,** although they may work the calculations with an **Underwriting Interest Rate** 1% to 2% higher than your **Initial Rate,** in order to reassure themselves that you can actually handle the payments that will be coming up.

See also **Ratio** and **Qualifying.**

Tip: Loan Advisors have several methods of working around these Ratios. One of their favorites is to have you pay off other debts, so you can qualify for a larger Loan Amount with them. This often makes sense, as home loans are usually at better Rates than other debts, and are tax deductible.

Always ask what the lenders Borrower Qualifications are, and have your Loan Advisor write out all the elements of the formula that will be used to determine what amount you Qualify for. If you have a problem, ask what you can do "to bring your Ratios in line."

Bridge Loan—Also known as a **"Swing Loan."** If you're ready to buy a home, but your old home hasn't yet sold, the lender may sometimes offer to finance your **Downpayment** with a loan against your old home, to be paid off when it sells.

Trap: A Bridge Loan is not only expensive, it's dangerous. Even if your old home has several people talking about making offers, don't do it unless you know you can make both payments for several months. Offers have a way of evaporating, particularly if a buyer finds out you're under the gun to sell.

Bullet Loan—See also **Balloon Payment, Construction Loan,** and **Second Mortgage.**

Buyups/Buydowns—Arrangements with a lender to reduce either your **Origination** (or **Discount**) **Fee** or your **Rate.**

A borrower will often agree to a **Buyup** by paying more on the monthlies in order to have a lower (or **Zero**) **Origination Fee.**

Sometimes developers or sellers will **Buydown** the monthly payment for a set period of time by paying more **Fees** along with the borrower's **Origination Fee.**

See also **Zero Point/Cost Loans.**

Cap, Lifetime—See **Lifetime Cap.**

Cap, Payment—See **Payment Cap.**

Cash Out Refinance—A **Refinance** that allows you to take **Cash Out** of your **Equity** in your home. Because these loans had particularly high foreclosure rates during the early 90's, many lenders either won't do them, or will do them only with higher **Interest Rates.**

If you've built up significant **Equity,** you have a good place to put your **Cash Out** dollars elsewhere, and if you can manage the higher payments, a **Cash Out Refinance** often makes sense, because it's usually tax deductible, and the **Rates** are often lower than any other kind of loan.

 Trap: Watch out for high, upfront Fees that can zap your Cash Out funds.

CLO (Computerized Loan Origination)—This term originally meant a **Loan Advisor** keying your **Loan Application** directly into a lender's software program that could recommend a **Loan Program,** evaluate your **Credit Report,** and do much of the paperwork involved with **Processing** and **Underwriting.**

It has now been extended to mean your filling out your own **Loan Application Online,** and getting the same recommendations and evaluations directly from the lender's computer. Doing your own entry obviously cuts time and some of the big **Online Application Mortgage Brokers** will cut their **Fees** for your doing everything on the **CLO** program.

See also **Application, Online Applications,** and the **National Money$ource Directory** in the **Appendix.**

Closing—Also called the **"Settlement."** The moment in time when the lender provides **Funding,** and the loan goes on **Record** against your home. If this is a **Purchase,** this is the also when your home **Title** transfers to your name. This moment is often preceded by a meeting which has also come to be called the **Closing,** where the **Escrow Company,** or whoever is insuring the **Title,** makes certain all points of the deal are agreed upon and signed, and all cash needed for your **Downpayment** and **Closing Costs** has been paid and then allocated to the proper parties.

Depending on the tradition in your area, the deal, and the amount of the paperwork you've been able to review and negotiate ahead of time, this session can vary from a casual half hour, with a **Closing** person simply handing you reams of papers to sign, to a heated battle of last minute deal points between buyer and seller, their **Lawyers,** their real estate brokers, the **Escrow/Title Company,** and the **Loan Advisor.**

See also **Timing Your Close** for tips on saving money.

Closing Costs—Also called **"Settlement Costs."** Detailed on the **Closing Statement** (see below). The biggest item on this list for the borrower should be the **Origination Fee** charged by the lender.

Institutions often tack on service charges above the **Origination Fee.** We've seen lenders' service charges add up to more than the **Origination Fee.**

There are always additional charges from appraisers, **Escrow/Title** companies, **Lawyers,** property inspectors and other advisors. If at all possible, get a written quote on **Fees** from all of these people before you hire them to help you. Sometimes sellers will agree to pay some of the borrower's **Closing Costs** as part of the negotiations.

Closing Statement—Also called the **"Settlement Statement"** or the **"HUD-1"** or the **"HUD-1a,"** a U.S. Department of Housing and Urban Development prescribed form listing all the **Closing Costs** you pay for the **Purchase** (the **HUD-1**) or the **Refinance** (the **HUD-1a**). The form also itemizes costs paid for you by other parties (most commonly the seller).

Clouds on the Title—See **Title Report.**

COFI (Costs of Funds Index)—A common, national underlying **Adjustable Loan Index,** even though it's based only on the **Cost of Funds** in the 11th U.S. Treasury District on the West Coast. Although reputed to be the slowest moving **Index,** and therefore the least likely to hit you with a big increase in your monthly payment, the 11th District has recently changed its formula for tracking the **Index.** It may no longer be distinctly slower than other **Indices.**

See also **Index.**

Commitment—The formal written agreement on the part of the lender that they'll issue you a certain **Loan Amount** at a specific **Rate.** This document means you've passed their **Credit Check** and **Qualify** for the right **Loan Amount,** but often they haven't yet gotten the **Appraisal.** Be sure to ask what are the other hurdles you'll need to clear before they okay **Funding** of the loan. Also ask how long this process should take.

Comparables/Comps—A detailed list of home sales that are used in the **Appraisal** as the most important data to support **Market Value.** Lenders want three things with valid **Comps:**

1. The more recent the better, and nothing older than six months, as lenders consider anything older as not indicative of where the market is gong.

2. The same neighborhood.

3. The same type (i.e., single family, condo, etc.) of home.

When there haven't been enough sales within the last six months to meet these criteria, appraisers sometimes use other nearby **Comparable** neighborhoods with similar demographics, but this decision has to be explained in the **Appraisal**. See also **Market Value**.

Computerized Loan Origination—See CLO.

Conforming/Non Conforming Loans— that "Conform" to the guidelines set up by the large national mortgage stock market (the **Secondary Market**). The near collapse of the U.S. savings and loan (S&L) industry at the end of the 80's was forestalled somewhat by vast government shoring-up programs, but even more by the emergence of the stock market as a place to raise mortgage money and trade the financial paper just like bonds are traded.

While savings and loan companies continue to talk to borrowers and **"Originate"** loans (along with commercial banks and an array of other types of lenders), most of the mortgages offered to homeowners today don't come from the money in someone else's savings account.

The money comes from special stocks **Funded** in the **Secondary Market**. These giant pools will only **Fund First Mortgages** that conform to certain guidelines, which include maximum **Loan Amounts**, maximum **LTV, "A" Credit** borrowers, and easily appraised homes.

Non Conforming Loans are loans where **Conforming** guidelines are not met.

Typically they are for larger **Loan Amounts.** They're called **Jumbos** and sold in different **Secondary Market** pools without government insurance, so their **Interest Rate** is usually a little higher.

See also **Jumbo**.

Construction Loans—Also called a "Short-Term" or "Interim" loan. This loan helps you build a new home. Lenders, however, are notoriously shortsighted on the value of something that exists only on paper, particularly if you're doing much of the work yourself.

The result is that no lenders make standard **30-Year Fixed** or **Adjustable** loans on a "to be built" property. First, you get a **Construction Loan** or pay for the land and construction yourself some other way, usually by taking a **Home Equity Loan** against your existing home or by using your savings. Once the construction is complete, you can then **Refinance** your new home with **Take Out Financing,** typically, a standard **Fixed** or **Adjustable.**

Tip: As you put together your dream home plans, evaluate your possible funding sources as carefully as your architect, and, unless you're in a position to self finance, never start buying the land until you get a lender's commitment to the project.

Tip: The best way to find a **Construction Loan** is to browse sites in a location where an overall master developer is selling lots or where many other new homes (or new vacation homes) have already been **Financed**. Developers, builders, and kit home suppliers in such locations can help you find a **Construction Loan**. Or see if you can find local owner-builder classes, with newsletters that list local lenders. You can also find some **Construction Lenders** on the Internet. See the **National Money$ource Directory** in the **Appendix**.

A **Construction Loan** is often issued in stages, i.e., a first amount to help buy the land, a second to fund the first part of construction, a third for final construction, etc. They are often **Interest Only,** with a **Bullet** coming due within three months to year, when you are also supposed to be finished with construction.

See also **Subordinate Loan** and **Two-Close Loan.**

Tip: Try to avoid lenders that insist you get another lender to do the **Take Out Financing** when construction is finished and their loan comes to an end. This forces a **Two Close** situation that has higher closing costs. Keep looking for a lender that will allow an automatic **Rollover**

*of the **Construction Loan** into a 30-Year **Mortgage**. Their **Rate** may be higher, but you'll save on **Closing Costs**... and peace of mind.*

Conventional Loan—Any loan not insured through the **Federal Housing Administration (FHA)** or the **Veterans Administration (VA)**. A **Conventional Loan** may be either **Conforming** or **Non Conforming**. Despite the name, a large percentage of U.S. home loans in the 90's are *not* **Conventional Loans,** because the **FHA** or **VA Loans** have better **Rates** (for borrowers), and they sell better in the **Secondary Market** (which makes the lenders happy).

FHA and **VA Loans** have more restrictions, however, and they have extra paper work that has to be completed, so they usually take longer.

*Tip: Many **Loan Advisors** get better commissions from selling **Conventional Loans**, so these are the ones they suggest first. For the best **Rate**, look for a **Conforming, FHA Loan**. For the most flexibility, look for a **Non Conforming, Conventional Loan**. The most flexible **Loan Programs** of all are usually with lenders who **Portfolio** their loans, don't sell them on the **Secondary Market**, but raise the money in other ways, and keep the mortgages in their own Portfolio.*

Convertible Loan—A **Convertible Loan** starts out either **Fixed** or **Adjustable,** then, after several years, switches to the alternative program. The advantage of a **Fixed** switching to an **Adjustable** is a lower monthly payment than a **Fixed Rate,** because the lender can sell it on the **Secondary Market** as an **Adjustable**. This type of loan switches automatically at a given date in the future, and will have a new **Rate** determined by the **Index** at that time.

The advantage of an **Adjustable** switching to a **Fixed** is also lower payments at the outset, but you have the security of knowing that you'll have a "window" later when you can switch to a **Fixed Rate**. That **Rate** will also be determined by the **Index** during the period of time you can switch, but you can decide whether or not you want to switch. It's a good idea to go **Online** and check **Rates** (or subscribe to a **Rate Watch Service**) when you get into your **Rate** switch "window."

Co-Signing—Also called "Co-Making" and "Endorsement." Someone signing the loan along with the actual borrower, who agrees to be equally responsible that the loan will be paid off. Most often used when the borrower does not have a **Credit** history longer than two years or there are serious (but past) **Dings** on the borrower's **Credit Report.**

Cost of Funds Index—See **COFI.**

Creative Financing—A wide variety (and constantly growing) of financing techniques. The most common involve financing that allows a borrower to **Purchase** with little or no **Downpayment.** Typically, the seller either **Carries Back** a large **Second,** and/or credits back money from the **Downpayment** towards repairs or capital improvements the buyer promises to make some time in the future.
See also **Second, Seller Carryback** and **Wraparound.**

*Trap: Many lenders frown on various **Creative Financing** strategies, and loans often have clauses defining them as reason for **Foreclosure** and/or legal prosecution. Sellers often only agree to help with **Creative Financing** if the **Purchase Price** is higher than the market or when money is hard to find, and nothing is selling.*
If you're thinking about this kind of transaction—as either a buyer or a seller—make certain you understand the legality of the situation and the worst thing the lender can do to you if something goes wrong and either the buyer or the seller doesn't live up to his or her promises.

*Tip: When money is easily available, lenders are much more tolerant of **Seller Seconds**, and even offer **Zero Down** loans themselves (particularly to **First-Time Homebuyers**). If you need help with the **Downpayment**, always check current lender policies before you structure your purchase.*

Credit Rating—Along with a **Credit Report**, many lenders determine your **Credit Rating** on scales weighing how long you've been at a job, how often you've had credit checks from other financial institutions, etc. The best known of these evaluations are outsourced to Fair Isaac Scoring Service, which rates prospects on their **FICO** scale. They do not divulge to public what the elements are on their **Ratings.**

Credit Report—Ordered by the lender from one or more of the large, national credit agencies like Experian (was TRW), Equifax (CBI), or Trans Union to verify your sources of income and   payment history. We recommend your getting your own **Report** by mail with the sample letter in the **Appendix,** or an **Online Service** that will get all three reports at once. See **Credit Reports** in the Supplemental Services section of our **National Money$ource Directory.**

If you have credit problems, start with your **Report,** then talk to a Consumer Credit Counseling Service. This nonprofit organization has offices around the country, which can give you specific information on how to go about re-establishing your credit. Call 800 388-2227 for the office nearest you.

Deed/Note—Also called "Mortgage **Deed,**" "**Deed of Trust,**" "Security **Deed,**" "Promissory **Note,**" and/or "Mortgage **Note.**" The most important of the formal **Loan Agreements** you must sign—and should receive a copy of—at the **Closing.** In some states, you have both a **Deed** and a **Note.**

Whatever the document is called, it should detail every aspect of your **Loan Program** and your promise to repay it. These documents used to be in minuscule type, archaic language, and go on for 40 pages. They're still long, but they must be legible sized type, and most lenders have improved their clarity in describing the **Loan Payment Schedule** and other vital facts on your loan.

Deed in Lieu of Foreclosure—If you ever get stuck in the nightmare situation where you can no longer make your monthly mortgage payment and values in your neighborhood have gone down to the point that the property is not worth the amount of loan against it, you need to notify the lender about the situation, and try to obtain a **Forbearance** or **Workout Agreement,** or—if you have no hope of regaining a financial situation where you can salvage your ownership—ask them to accept a **Deed in Lieu of Foreclosure**. Such a **Deed** gives the lender all ownership rights in exchange for not going through a legal **Foreclosure** procedure against you. This saves the lender legal costs, and saves your having a **Foreclosure** go against your **Credit Rating**.

When the recession hit large communities in the 90's, many desperate homeowners found themselves participating in a gruesome ritual known as "Mailing Back the Keys," i.e., simply filling out a **Deed in Lieu** form, and sending it with the house keys back to the lender.

Lenders hate such informality. Some will accept such **Deeds,** if an entire community has been blighted, but others will go ahead with the **Foreclosure,** no matter what the expense. This is particularly true if your loan has a **Recourse** clause allowing them to sue you for any costs above the amount they receive from the **Foreclosure** sale.

If you have the resources to fight the **Foreclosure,** you may postpone some of the procedure by filing a **Homestead** on your property, or a bankruptcy. See an attorney specializing in these actions.

See also **Foreclosure, Forbearance, Homestead** and **Recourse.**

Default—Failure to comply with one or more of the essential clauses of your mortgage agreement, including not making your monthly payment.

Several other lesser known clauses—such as causing "waste" to the property (failure to keep it up), not living in it as a primary residence, not notifying the lender of a sale (see **Due on Sale** and **Wraparound**), not keeping proper insurance, or not paying the **Real Estate Taxes**—can also cause you to be in **Default** and the lender to start foreclosure proceedings. Obviously, it's crucial to read these clauses carefully when as you're evaluating a loan.

Demand—See **Payoff.**

Depreciation—When your home's **Market Value** goes down. This can happen either because of poor maintenance, neighborhood changes, or a drop in the economy that affects all homes.

Dings on Your Credit—If you're one of about 70% of today's loan applicants, you eventually get a call from your **Loan Advisor** saying there are a few problems. You've got **Dings on Your Credit.** This may be anything from having forgotten a single Sears Credit Card installment payment to a full-blown bankruptcy.

If you've already gotten a copy of your **Credit Report** ahead of time, as we recommend, you'll know about these before you make your **Application.** Always tell your **Loan Advisor** about major **Dings**—including missed home loan payments—ahead of time. The problem may disqualify you from the loan, but you *must* know this as soon as possible— knowing you're disqualified means you have time to shop for another lender.

*Tip: If there's a problem, ask your **Loan Advisor** what you can do about it. Often all you need is a simple **Letter of Explanation** stating "I was late on the (date, description) payment because (reason)." Even if your reason was the payment dropped behind the kitchen cabinet and you didn't know it was lost until you received the notice, as long as you don't have a pattern of delinquencies, a **Letter of Explanation** can clear a minor **Ding.***

*If you've got a major problem and the lender you're talking to can't clear you, ask which lender they'd suggest you call. They may be able to recommend lenders which specialize in "B," "C," and even "D" **Credit** bor-*

*rowers. These lenders provide lower **LTV Loan Amounts**, and they charge higher **Rates**, but they do have **Funds** available.*

Disclosure—Lenders are required by several federal laws, including **Truth In Lending** and the **Real Estate Settlement Procedures Act (RESPA)**, to disclose how much your loan is going to cost you. These **Disclosures** begin when they give you the **APR,** which adds the **Origination Fee** and other **Closing Costs** into the first year's **Interest Rate.**

Upon first talking with you or, at the latest, upon receipt of your **Application,** the lender is required to send you an initial **TIL (Truth in Lending)** or **TALC (Total Annual Loan Cost** for **Reverse Mortgages)** sheet.

Along with several generic brochures describing possible costs and disclosing possible **Affiliations** with title, insurance, and other related companies, this **"Good Faith Estimate" Disclosure** includes a form stating specifically the **Interest Rate,** the initial monthly payments, the "Worst Case Scenario" highest monthly payments you can have with the **Loan Program,** and—sit down when you read this—the total amount the loan will cost you if kept until fully paid off.

*Tip: Unless you pay to have a **Lock In** on your **Rate**, all these numbers can change because this is only a **Good Faith Estimate**. Always ask your **Loan Advisor** if the **Rate** market is volatile, or if the **Estimate** might change radically because **Program Qualifications** are particularly stringent, and you're likely to have to change **Programs**.*

*Trap: We've known **Loan Advisors** who habitually give **TIL's** with a low **Rate Program** that practically no borrower **Qualifies** for, then pull a **Bait and Switch** later, when you don't have time to get another loan.*

*Always **Double App** when you're going with a lender with an exceptionally low **Rate**, particularly if you've got a **Mortgage Broker** working with an outside lender, who might not be telling the **Broker** when they're about to drop a **Program**.*

The **TIL** also has a checkoff list of the other important **Terms** of the loan, i.e., whether or not this is a **Fixed Rate** loan, has a **Prepay Penalty** and/or a **Balloon Payment.**

The most important **Disclosures** are given to you at the **Closing,** when you should receive the **Note** and/or the **Deed,** plus the **Closing Statement** listing all the **Fees** due the lender and the others getting paid in connection with your **Purchase** or **Refinance.** By law, you have three days to review these costs, and you may decide to rescind the loan at that time.

> *Tip: These **Disclosures** look as uninteresting as a stock prospectus, but fortunately they're shorter and are required to be written in more or less plain English. Take the time to review them. If they're ok at the outset, file for future reference, both when you go to the **Closing** and down the road when your **Loan Payment Schedule** changes.*

> *Trap: In some areas, the final **Closing** or **Settlement** is not required to be a meeting. If the meeting is not required, the lender is not required to give you the **Closing Statement** in advance, and you may loose your right to recision. Always insist on a **Closing** meeting and the opportunity to review the **Closing Statement**.*

This system should be adequate protection against your getting into a loan with unexpected costs. Unfortunately, vital information, like the actual **Interest Rate** you end up with or the total of miscellaneous **Fees** you have to pay, is often misquoted or omitted in the preliminary **Disclosures**.

You rarely have the time to carefully review and comprehend these forms. They're often handed to you with the request to approve immediately. We've even seen **Closings** where borrowers didn't even get copies of all their **Disclosures** and **Loan Agreements** until they were specifically requested.

The easiest to understand and most complete of the forms, the **Closing Statement,** is only available at the very end of the process, when you've expended so much energy in getting the loan, you're very reluctant to turn it down, even if you are fully aware of your right of recision. We've rescinded loans when the lender came up with a loan that was grossly different from what was promised, but only very rarely, and only when we had a **Double App** loan waiting.

Discount Fee—Usually added in to the **Origination Fee** and/or **Points.** A **Fee** the lender charges to discount the **Start Rate** on **Adjustable Loan** payments. Rarely available on **Fixed Rate** loans. Usually runs 1% to 4% of the **Loan Amount,** depending on how much lower your **Start Rate** is.

Documentation—Also called the "**Application** Package," the "Complete Package," and the "Loan Docs." Along with your **Application** questionnaire, a salaried employee will—at minimum—need to submit a current pay stub and signed requests for verifications of **Downpayment,** other income, and employment. A self-employed or a commissioned person will also need tax returns for several years.

In addition to your own paperwork, the lender will ask you or your agent to have a **Title Report** sent to them. They'll order a copy of your **Credit Report** and need you and the seller to help in arranging the **Appraisal.** All of these pieces of paper become part of your **Documentation.**

Start assembling all these papers as early as possible, so that if a tax return or other vital document is missing from where you thought it was, you can retrieve a copy from someplace else.

 *Tip: If assembling **Documentation** proves very difficult for one reason or another, check with your **Loan Advisor.** When money is easily available, you often can get a **Low-Doc** or a **No-Doc Loan** if you pay higher **Fees.***

Double App—Making a complete **Application** to more than one lender at a time. Your most potent weapon against a lender's charging you huge **Fees** at the **Closing** and/or changing **Rates** or **Programs** on you at the last minute.

Lenders discourage this savvy hunting strategy, and you usually have to take the time to find two **Loan Advisors** and most probably will have to pay some double **Application and Appraisal Fees.** Nevertheless, we recommend it unless you're working with a **Loan Advisor** who has a very strong local reputation of always performing as promised.

Downpayment—The amount of the **Purchase Price** that you pay in cash. Lenders will want to be able to check your source of the **Downpayment,** and showing them the money in a bank account you just opened a week ago isn't good enough. They want to be sure the money is really yours and not borrowed from someone else.

If you haven't had the money in a verifiable account for some time, you'll often have to write a **Letter of Explanation** detailing the source, i.e., that the money is coming from the sale of your old residence, or is a non returnable gift from your parents, or whatever.

See also **LTV.**

Due on Sale Clause—Sometimes money is tight when you're selling your home, and the new buyer would like to keep the old mortgage instead of applying for a new one. Although a few older loans allow unrestricted **Assumption,** most have **Due on Sale** clauses that allow the mortgage holder to foreclose if they find out about a sale accomplished without their approval.

*Tip: By law, most loans with a **Prepayment Penalty** must allow **Assumption.** The law does not prescribe how much the lender may charge for the privilege, however, nor does it restrict how the lender may define the creditworthiness needed for **Assumption.***

*Trap: Unless you know the buyer is arranging for a new loan within six months or less, insist on getting lender's approval of the **Assumption.** If a lender collects on a **Due on Sale Foreclosure,** they may go after you for damages, because you were the borrower who originally made the **Loan Agreement** with them.*

Equity—The value of your ownership in your home. For example, suppose you bought a $100,000 home with a $10,000 **Downpayment** and a $90,000 loan. Subsequently you've added in another $10,000 as the **Amortization** part of your monthly payments, and the value of your home has **Appreciated** yet another $20,000 in **Market Value.** Now your home's total **Market Value** would be $120,000, the loan would be down to $80,000, and your present **Equity** (including **Appreciation**) would be $40,000—33% ($40,000 divided by $120,000).

 *Tip: You'll particularly need to track these calculations if you want your lender to stop collecting **PMI** and/ or tax/insurance **Escrow** payments. As your **Equity** increases, you may also want to **Refinance** or get a **Home Equity Second.***

Equity Fee—Used mainly with **Reverse Mortgages,** the **Equity Fee** allows lenders to add a percentage of your home's **Market Value** into the **Loan Amount** due. This **Fee**—which can be a whopping 5% or 10% of the property's **Market Value**—has a significant impact on how much you or your estate has to pay back. Because it often occurs outside the regular **Disclosure** dates, however, it can easily be overlooked as you review the **Truth in Lending TALC Disclosures** the lender is required to give you.

 *Tip: Always ask for complete explanations and a careful walkthrough on the **Maximum Payment Scenario** (see the **Appendix**) when a **Loan Advisor** mentions unusual changes in **Equity, Principal,** or **Amortization.** A larger **Loan Amount** not only means more money needing to be paid back but also a larger amount you're paying **Interest** on.*

Equity Second—Also called **Home Equity Loan** or **Home Equity Line of Credit (HELOC)**. More often extended by the lenders who do credit cards and car loans than those who do **Firsts,** these loans are designed to let you tap the **Equity** dollars in your home after you've owned it for a while with a minimum of hassle.

Letters often arrive at your doorstep offering "no **Points,**" **Interest Rates** lower than most credit cards, and dollar amounts over 100% of your home's value.

If you need cash for a possible expenditure that you can repay fairly quickly, they may make more monetary sense than any other kind of revolving line of credit, because not only should the **Rate** be better, but they are often tax deductible.

If you have a large necessary expenditure like replacing your roof, putting someone through college, or large, ongoing health bills that you cannot repay quickly, you can probably get a better deal with a **Second** from the lender that made your **First Mortgage,** or some other standard mortgage lender, who can do a **Fixed Rate** over an extended period of time, usually 15 or 20 years.

See also **Second Mortgage** and **Seller Carryback.**

Trap: Be aware that *Equity Seconds* can have several pitfalls:

1. They may have *Fees* that are not clearly *Disclosed* on the *Application.*

2. The introductory *Rate* is often a *Teaser* that disappears after six to nine months, and the "actual" *Rate* used for the balance of the time you borrow the money can be as high as 21%. Whatever the "actual" *Rate* might be at the outset, it will fluctuate because these loans rarely have a *Fixed Rate.* Instead they vary from month to month with an underlying *Index.*

3. The *Amortization Schedule* on *Equity Seconds* is usually short (five to seven years). This translates into a higher monthly payment than is standard for *30-Year Mortgage* of the same amount. Be sure to always check the actual dollar amounts of your monthly payments.

Escrow Account—The account where a neutral third party holds all deposits from the various parties in the **Pur-**

chase or **Refinance.** More and more states are recognizing the services of **Escrow** and **Title** companies to process these funds, provide **Title Insurance,** and otherwise facilitate the transaction.

In many areas, however, **Escrows** are handled by real estate brokers and/or **Lawyers.** This may become a problem. We've had a shady real estate broker hold a substantial deposit for more than two *years* after the deal fell apart.

*Tip: If you are a newcomer to an area, and the **Escrow** holder is not bonded or seems unreliable in any way, see if you can't make arrangements for the deposits to be held by a bank or some other third party whose trustworthiness can be more easily verified.*

Escrow/Title Company—In some states these companies are licensed to research the "Chain of Title," issue a **Title Report,** make sure the legal seller is conducting the transaction, **Record** the transaction when it is legally completed, and insure that all the loans, easements, and ownership of the property have been disclosed.

They can hold the **Good Faith Deposit** from the buyer, add the **Downpayment** from the buyer and the moneys from any **First** or **Second** mortgages, pay off any old loans, the **Real Estate Taxes,** and **Insurance,** the real estate agent's commission, etc., then remit the remainder to the seller.

In locations where the buyer pays the majority of **Escrow/Title Fees,** check with at least three companies to find out what their services and **Fees** are before you hire one. If your state has **Lawyers** doing these tasks, it's probably best to interview four or five. You can save $700–$800 in **Fees** on the **Purchase** of a $100,000 home.

In a **Refinance,** you will also have-to-have the "Chain of Title" insured for the new lender, so the **Refi** transaction is usually handled by a **Escrow/Title Company,** as well.

Family Debt— The second **Borrower Qualification Ratio** that lenders take into consideration when they're calculating how much money they'll loan you. Lenders set their **Ratios** as percentages of your total annual income for:

1. **PITI** The percentage allowed for spending on your housing costs.

2. **Family Debt** The percentage allowed for all other recurring debt, including costs for car and student loans, partially paid credit cards, etc.

See also **PITI** and review the **Loan Amount Qualifying Worksheet** in the **Appendix** for the **Ratio** formulas.

Fee/Fees—Charges for various services needed to obtain your loan.

See also **Application, Appraisal, Assumption, AUS, Closing Costs, Lock In, Origination Fee,** and **Underwriting Fee** for more details on the major charges, and **Disclosures** for various government required forms that will help you find out about and track these expenses.

FHA/VA Loans—Because **FHA (Federal Housing Authority) Loans** and **VA (Veterans Administration) Loans** are guaranteed by the government, they usually have lower **Interest Rates** and **Fees** than **Conventional Loans.**

The disadvantages are that they have lower ceilings on dollar amounts and **Loan to Value** amounts, either of which may rule these loans out for you. They may have more stringent **Borrower Qualifications,** more paper work and a longer **Turnaround Time.** Finally, the **Loan Advisor** presenting the program may get a higher commission for a **Conventional Loan,** and be reluctant to work on **FHA** or **VA.**

If the **Loan Amount** available for the government-insured loans works for you, be persistent working to get an **FHA** or **VA,** even if you don't appear to **Qualify** at first. Ask if they allow **Seconds,** how to change your payment **Ratios** to meet **Borrower Qualifications,** etc. Your thorough research can win you a **Fixed** at a low **Rate** that will be a particular joy whenever inflation hits again.

See also **VA.**

FICO Rating—See **Credit Rating.**

Financing—This can refer either to the **Financing** process that the borrower goes through, or the **Financing** that the lender does in order to sell your loan on the **Secondary Market.**

The **Secondary Market** for U.S. home loans is a trillion dollar business. It attracts investment dollars because of the **Interest Rate** returns on the dollars invested. The **Origination** lender you talk to when you're making out your **Application** typically bundles it with others and "recycles" it by selling it to the investor pools in the **Secondary Market.**

The **Origination** lender then goes back to what it does best—**Originating** loans.

See also **Secondary Market, Origination,** and **Servicing.**

First Mortgage—Often simply called the **First.** This loan is usually extended by a large, institutional lender. It is typically **Amortized** over a **30-Years**, and bears **Interest** on a **Fixed** or an **Adjustable Rate Schedule.** The contracts detailing your pledge of your home as security and how and when you'll pay the loan back are typically called a "Mortgage **Note,**" a "Promissory **Note,**" and/or a **"Deed of Trust."**

First-Time Homebuyer Programs—Government **Loan Programs,** both national and local, to help you get your first home. These range from special tax credits to outright grants.

See also **MCC Tax Credits, Neighborhood Advantage Loans,** and **VA.**

 *Tip: Take a look at the Fannie Mae Homepath web site at www.homepath.com or call 800 732-6643 for an overview of **Programs** and telephone numbers of local **Loan Advisors.***

Fixed Mortgage—Also called a **Fixed** or a **FRM (Fixed Rate Mortgage).** The classic **First Mortgage** our parents knew and loved. Usually has a **30-Year Amortization**

Schedule. It worked fine until inflation drove payments out of sight. In the early 80's, the **Fixed Rates** jumped over the 15% mark. Today they're back below 10%, offering the best route for anyone figuring on staying in a home more than five years.
See also **15-Year / 30-Year / 40-Year Fixed.**

Flood Certification—Federal map verification done for the lender, stating whether or not the property is located in an area requiring **Flood Insurance**. Because area ratings change from time to time, most lenders require new **Flood Certificates** for each loan they do, even if they're doing a **Refi** on a property that was **Certified** as not requiring **Flood Insurance** only a few years before. There is often a **Flood Certification Fee** included in your **Closing Costs.**

Flood Insurance—Required by the government insured **FHA/VA Loans,** and by the **Secondary Market** whenever a property is inside a Special Flood Hazard Area (SFHA) specifically designated on national FEMA (Federal Emergency Management Agency) maps as likely to have floods.
These maps are updated from time to time—when there's a flood or more stress is put on local sewers, your rating goes up. When your local government strengthens the levy system, or reroutes a waterway, your rating goes down.
Ratings on all but the lowest levels require SFHA coverage, although FEMA encourages you to get it anyway, just for safety's sake. Some communities which have never had serious flooding don't participate in the program and aren't rated at all.
For all SFHA areas, the lender will require you to have a full year's policy at the time your new loan goes in place, and the premium will be one of your **Closing Costs.**
See also **Hazard Insurance.**

 *Trap: Your lender may offer you **Flood Insurance** with an **Affiliated Company,** but always check with your **Hazard Insurance** agent as to whether or not you need **Flood Insurance,** and—if they can do a policy for you— how much they'll charge. Typically, they'll be cheaper than the insurer recommended by the lender.*

Make sure to ask what **Rate** your home has (it will vary according to the map in existence at the time your home was built), and how much you need in coverage.

FEMA usually requires either the smaller of the **Loan Amount** or the amount equaling the total replacement of the building, which—importantly in many upscale locations—does not include the **Market Value** of the land. The lender might insist on being covered for the full **Loan Amount,** but should never insist on full **Market Value** of the property.

 Tip: You can reach FEMA to obtain local information at 800 358-9616, or 800 427-2297 or check their site at www.fema.gov.

Floor, Lifetime—See **Lifetime Floor.**

Floor, Payment—See **Payment Floor.**

Forbearance Agreement—Also known as a **Workout Agreement.** A lender's agreeing to accept a lower monthly mortgage payment from a borrower who's in financial trouble, but can demonstrate that the problem will right itself in the foreseeable future.

See also **Foreclosure.**

Foreclosure—The legal procedure whereby the lender sues you for not upholding the **Terms** of your loan, and wins the right to sell your home to recover their **Loan Amount** and any **Foreclosure** legal costs. Usually this action is for failing to make your monthly payments, but you can also have a **Foreclosure** started against you for not paying your taxes, keeping up the property, or **Defaults** against other **Terms** of your loan.

See also **Default** and **Homestead.**

 Tip: As soon as you realize you will not be able to make payments, get in touch with your lender with an honest description of the situation. If you've just been in a car wreck, a flood, or some other disaster, and you believe you'll be back at work and making payments within

BY CLYDE AND SHARI STEINER

*the foreseeable future (get your doctor and employer verification, here), you may be able to get them to grant you a **Forbearance** or **Workout Agreement**, whereby they allow lower monthly payments for a fixed period of time.*

*Trap: Many states have **Homestead** laws that are supposed to allow you to protect your home from **Foreclosure** by registration. Unfortunately, most lenders have **Foreclosure** procedures that eventually get around a **Homestead** registration, and, once you've registered a **Homestead**, it is very difficult to do a **Refinance**.*

*Trap: Some home loans and most **Home Equity** and **Construction Loans** have a **Recourse** clause, which allows the lender to go after you personally for repayment of the loan and their **Foreclosure** costs, if the sale of your home does not suffice. Avoiding loans with such clauses is usually difficult, because in areas where they are prevalent, nearly all lenders use them.*

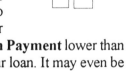

Fully Amortized Payment—With **Negative Amortization Mortgage,** your monthly payments are structured so that the lender gets their interest first, then the rest of the payment goes to **Principal**. If **Rates** go up steeply, your **Stepup Cap** may keep your **Minimum Payment** lower than what is needed to **Fully Amortize** your loan. It may even be less than enough to pay the interest due.

This structure keeps your monthly payment more affordable, but results in **Negative Amortization,** i.e., the **Principal** *grows* each month, instead of getting smaller.

See also **Negative Amortization.**

Fully Indexed Start Rate—Also called a "True" **Start Rate.** An **Adjustable Loan** where the first payments reflect all the underlying **Indices** and **Margins** in contrast to a **Teaser Start Rate.**

Fund/Funding—When a loan **Closes,** large numbers of dollars are transferred from the new lender to almost everyone involved with the **Purchase** or **Refinance** except you (unless you're doing a **Cash Out Refinance**). Today, most lenders can give you a three or four week "Window" when they can provide this **Funding,** once they've completed **Underwriting** your loan and are sure that you and the property confirm with the **Loan Program** requirements. If your loan is for a **Purchase,** with a specific deadline for **Closing,** knowing how fast a lender can **Fund** is one of the crucial pieces of information about their **Programs.**

*Trap: Always ask about a lender's **Funding** capabilities when you're interviewing **Loan Advisors**. Since the advent of the **Secondary Market**, lenders are much less likely than they used to be to run out of **Funds**, but it does still happen. Some lenders can also sometimes take unusually long—ten days to two weeks—after completing **Underwriting**, and sending you your **Approval** to make the **Funds** available.*

Garbage Fees—A term regarding all the **Fees** lenders are now adding to your **Closing Costs.** Sometimes used by a real estate agent disgusted with the service a client is getting from a lender, or a **Loan Advisor** knocking someone else's **Loan Program.**

Good Faith Deposit—A deposit by the buyer to an **Escrow Account** to verify to the property seller that the offer being made is serious, and will be accomplished according to the terms of the **Purchase** contract.

Good Faith Estimate—The **Disclosure** a lender is legally required to make to you when you make your **Application.** Part of the **TIL (Truth in Lending)** or **TALC (Total Annual Loan Calculation).** Includes details on how much a monthly payment will be and how much the total payments over the complete **30-Year** life of the loan will be. There's also a **Terms Checklist,** including whether or not the **Loan Program** is **Assumable** or has a **Prepay Penalty.**

If you make an **Application** to a **Mortgage Broker,** you may get two sets of these **Disclosures,** one from the **Mortgage Broker,** and one from the lender with the actual **Loan Program** you finally select. The one direct from the lender is the most important, and should be reviewed as you get ready for the **Closing.**

See also **TIL/TALC Disclosures.**

Hazard Insurance—This policy covers fire, acts of God (i.e., wind, rain, but often *not* earthquakes, hurricanes, and floods), vandalism, theft, and the third party liability associated with your home ownership. A prepaid year's policy is required by most lenders placing a new loan.

Tip: If you're buying a condo or co-op, the building may be covered separately from the contents of your unit. See your Homeowners Association for this information.

*Trap: As with **Flood Insurance,** your lender may offer you their own **Affiliated** company's **Hazard Insurance** coverage—and can force you to pay for it with your **Closing Costs,** if you don't provide your own policy. Always check with independent insurance agents as to what they'd charge to cover you.*

*Tip: If you're not sure where to begin insurance shopping, check with your real estate agent and your **Escrow/ Title Company.** Typically, an independent will be cheaper (we've seen them be as much as 50% cheaper) than the insurer recommended by the lender.*

*Find out from the lender how much coverage you'll be required to have. Most lenders only require building replacement coverage, which, importantly in many upscale locations, does not include the **Market Value** of the land.*

*The lender might insist on being covered for the full **Loan Amount,** but should not insist on coverage for full **Market Value** of the property, because the land will still be there, even if your home burns to the ground.*

Home Equity Loan / Line of Credit (HELOC)—See **Equity Second.**

Homestead—A legal procedure whereby you use a state law to register your home to protect it from **Foreclosure.** Although filing a **Homestead** or a bankruptcy should be investigated if you've run into a difficult financial situation, you should do so with the help of a real estate attorney, who can explain exactly what the action will mean to your credit in your state, and how much **Foreclosure** protection it offers against your specific mortgage situation. Many attorneys have told us most homes are only partially protected by a **Homestead.**

See also **Foreclosure.**

HUD-1/HUD-1A—See **Closing Statement.**

Impound Account—Also called a "Reserve" or "Trust" Account. On mortgages larger than 80% **Loan to Value,** lenders often want extra insurance that the loan won't have any problems, so they collect your prorated tax and house insurance payments along with your monthly mortgage payment, then disburse the money to the proper parties as they come due.

This may save you from last minute scrambling when **Real Estate Taxes** come due, but you lose the interest on the money you'd have had if you had put it aside yourself, and lenders' computers, unfortunately, have been known *not* to make the proper payments for you.

See also **PMI** as well as **Qualified Written Request** for how to complain about lender non-payments of your taxes and insurance.

 *Tip: Try to avoid the **LTV** that requires **Impound** payments. If you must start off with the higher **LTV**, find out how to have the payment dropped after your loan payments have reduced the **Principal Amount** below the 80% **LTV** level, and **PMI** should no longer be required.*

Index—The base **Rate** which causes an **Adjustable Loan** to go up or down. Often the 6-month or 1-year Treasury bill, but can be more difficult to find **Indices,** like the **Cost of Funds Index (COFI)** or the **London Interbank Offer Rate (LIBOR).** Always ask where you can find a published source of your **Index,** and have your **Loan Advisor** show you charts on how volatile their **Index** is in comparison to the T-bill, the **COFI,** and others. The **COFI** has traditionally been the least volatile **Index.** An **Index** with a lot of spikes is more likely to be on the upswing cycle when your **Loan Payment Schedule** calls for a payment change.
See also **COFI** and **LIBOR.**

Initial Rate—The **Interest Rate** that sets your **Loan** payment for the first three to six months of an **Adjustable Loan.** This is at the **Rate** the lender advertises, and is sometimes steeply discounted as a **Teaser** to bring in lots of borrowers.
See also **Interest Rate** and **Teaser Rate.**

*Trap: Such loans will save you money at the outset, but are usually either **Neg Am** loans or **Adjustables** with exceptionally high **Lifetime** and **Payment Caps**. Be sure to ask if the **Start Rate** is a **Teaser** or a "True" or "Fully Indexed" Start Rate.*

Interest Only—Loans that are not **Amortized,** and require no payment of **Principal.** Common with **Construction Loans** and **Seller Carrybacks,** where the **Principal** is repaid in a lump sum at the end of the loan. **Negative Amortization** loans also sometimes offer **Interest Only** payment options.

Interest Rate—Often simply called "the **Rate.**" Your loan **Rate** determines your payment. It is based on an underlying **Index,** which often reflects the **Secondary Market's Cost of Funds** for the loan, plus a **Margin** of profit.

Although lenders are required to quote the **APR** as well as the **Interest Rate,** so that you know the first year's cost of your loan, the **Interest Rate** stays with the loan as long as you have it. With **Adjustables,** the **Interest Rate** changes from time to time according to your **Loan Payment Schedule.**

Because you pay off **Principal** as well as **Interest** with **Amortized** loans, you can't calculate your loan payments accurately without an **Amortization** function on your calculator or spread sheet.

 *Tip: In the **Appendix** you'll find a **Loan Payment Estimator** to determine the monthly and annual payments for a **Fixed, 30-Year Amortized** or a **Fixed, 15-Year Amortized** loan. You can also use one of the **Online Estimators** listed in our **National Money$ource Directory.***

Jumbo—Loans for amounts larger than the **Conforming** amount prescribed by the **Secondary Market.** Because these loans are not federally insured nor included in the largest **Secondary Market** pools, they usually carry a higher **Rate** and have a higher **Origination Fee.**

If you happen to be looking for what is often called a **Jumbo Jumbo** (usually defined as a **Loan Amount** above $700,000), however, be aware there are lenders like Chase who particularly want you as a client, and often offer particularly good **Rates** to get you. Be sure to review our **National Money$ource Directory** and search the Net for good deals tailored specifically to your situation.

Lawyer—Often used to write or review **Purchase** documents, go over loan papers, and inform you how the sales procedure works. In some states, **Lawyers** are the only ones licensed to research the "Chain of **Title**" to be sure a legal sale is being conducted.

In states where **Escrow/Title Companies** conduct the "Chain of **Title**" search, many residential **Purchases** and

Refis take place without a **Lawyer,** unless something out of the ordinary comes up and you need legal assistance.

Since **Lawyers** can be very expensive, whenever you need one, try to get a flat **Fee** quote on all costs to be incurred from at least four or five **Lawyers** before you hire one.

 *Tip: Preview the questions you have regarding your transaction with your real estate agent and your **Loan Advisor** before spending consulting time with your **Lawyer.***

Letter of Explanation—If you have **Dings** on your **Credit,** but the lender still thinks you may qualify for your loan, you'll be asked to send in a **Letter of Explanation.** Try to make the explanation as short and simple as possible. Lenders understand occasional mistakes, or problems due to illness or loss of a job, but they have no interest in more complex family matters behind the mistakes.

Letters of Explanation can also be requested for your source of **Downpayment,** past court cases, your self-employment record, or any other items that an **Underwriter** feels is unusual in your loan **Documentation.**

LIBOR (London InterBank Offer Rate)—A common U.S. **Adjustable Loan Index,** even though it's based on an international tracking system. Popular with the **Secondary Market** because it makes loans saleable internationally.

Life of Loan—Also called the loan **Term.** The length of time it takes to pay off the loan—typically, 30 years.

See also **Payoff** and **Term.**

Lifetime Cap—Your payment **"Ceiling,"** the most your payment **Rate** can go up during the life of the loan. Typically **Adjustables** can go up 5% to 8%.

On your follow-up interview, be sure to ask your **Loan Advisor** to give you the exact resulting percentages and

Maximum Payment Scenario on the loan they're proposing for you.

Lifetime Floor—The lowest **Rate** an **Adjustable Loan** can go. The **Floor** is set in the **Loan Agreement.** It used to be the same percentage amount below the **Start Rate** as the **Ceiling** was above, but since **Rates** have gone down in the 90's, that practice has changed.

*Tip: The **Floor** is not as dangerous to your pocketbook as the **Ceiling**, but when you're deciding between several different loans, check it anyway. If different **Loan Programs** are similar except for different **Floors,** go with the one that goes down the lowest.*

Loan Advisor—A vital key to a successful loanhunt is a **Loan Advisor** who lives up to his or her promises.

Look for **Advisors** who do the most lending in your area on your kind of property. Besides surveying our **National Money$ource Directory** and your local newspaper real estate sections for weekly **Rate** surveys and ads, ask your real estate agent, **Escrow/Title Company,** and **Lawyer** for recommendations.

*Trap: It used to be that only mortgage company **Loan Advisors** were trained as salespeople. **Loan Advisors** working for banks or savings and loans were largely paid-by-the-hour paper pushers, who were trained in the arts of seven ways to say "no."*

*Since the 80's, however, **Loan Advisors,** wherever they work, are usually commissioned salespeople who have been trained in at least seven ways to say "yes!"*

*The good ones are a big help overcoming **Qualification** problems, but don't expect to hear about the negative sides of their **Loan Program(s).** Always get an **Advisor** to send you a written description of their **Loan Program(s),** and read carefully before you decide which one to select.*

If you talk to a **Portfolio** lender's **Loan Advisor,** you get in-depth, complete information about a limited range of loans.

A **Loan Advisor** working as a **Mortgage Broker,** on the other hand, offers a wider range of loans and market perspective, but can make promises that don't materialize. They work with numerous lenders, and are often hooked up to computer networks that allow them to place your loan with lenders all over the country. Sometimes they charge a higher **Origination Fee** than the institution's **Loan Advisor** would, but often they don't.

A concerned, knowledgeable **Mortgage Broker** can save you much time interviewing and filling out papers... But a bad one can cost weeks of unsuccessful loan searching and thousands of dollars in worthless **Application Fees.**

Even if the first **Loan Advisor** you talk with seems knowledgeable, easy to work with, and offers you a **Loan Program** you like, it's savvy to continue to survey five to ten lenders or **Mortgage Brokers.** Once you've gotten a feel for the market, go back for more information from the sources of the three best **Loan Programs.**

Tip: Ask for:
1. Credentials—state license number, membership in lender and/or **Mortgage Broker** *associations, the Chamber of Commerce, etc.*
2. Referrals from other borrowers in situations like yours who can tell you about their experiences. Because of confidentiality, these are often difficult to obtain, so follow-up with questions about referrals from real estate agents or other professionals.
3. A description of how he or she works with a client.

Because lender reputation is so difficult to verify (even a Better Business Bureau check is often insufficient), we recommend the **Double App** if you're in a situation where the lender's performance, as promised, is critical.

See also **Mortgage Broker.**

Loan Agreement—The dossier of all the documents that you and the lender sign, which define your promises to each other about how your loan will be implemented. These vary from lender to lender, and from state to state. The most important are the **Deed** and/or the **Note** that you sign at the **Closing.**

 *Tip: Ask to have a draft of the **Deed** and **Note** to review ahead of time. Unfortunately, we don't see many lenders who will provide these, but some will. If you can review them in advance, you'll have a much better understanding of the **Loan Program** you're considering.*

Loan Amount—The crucial number derived from the **Borrower Ratio** and **Loan to Value** calculations. Your job is to be sure this number works both with your budget and with the homes you're previewing.

Loan Payment Schedule—Also called a **Rate Adjustment Schedule. Adjustable Loan** payment amounts change periodically according to the **Schedule** detailed in your **Loan Agreement.** Usually it's once a year or once every six months, however **Neg Am** loan payments may change from month to month, although the minimum *required* payment only changes every six months.

Ask your **Loan Advisor** what the **Payment Caps** are for each **Rate** change, and review whether or not you may run into a situation where your salary wouldn't cover the **Maximum Payment Scenario.** Use this information to fill in the **Loan Evaluation Checklist** in the **Appendix.**

The **Payment Schedule** will be constrained by **Caps** and **Floors** on both the payments and the **Lifetime Ceiling,** as well as what's happening to the **Index** your loan is tied to.

There is also the question as to whether or not this might be a **Recasting** payments, where the lender may change the payments without regard to the **Payment Cap.** The **Loan Payment Schedule** is set forth first in the **Good Faith Estimate** given to you right after you make your **Application,** and is most specifically detailed in the **Note** and **Deed of Trust Agreements** you receive at the **Closing.**

*Tip: Once you've obtained your loan, track what's happening with the payments on a **Loan Evaluation Checklist** from the **Appendix**, or use one of the software programs listed in the **National Money$ource Directory**. If the lender doesn't seem to be making the adjustments correctly, you can contact them, or have an outside auditor from a tracking service like Mortgage Monitor at 800 Audit-USA do it for you.*

Loan Program Name—Sometimes called "Loan Product." Because most lenders offer both **Adjustable** and **Fixed Loans,** with several variations of each, they keep track of the different loan characteristics with **Loan Program Names**. Write this **Name** down as you go over your **Loan Evaluation Checklist** so that when you call back with more questions, you're sure you're talking about the same **Loan Program.**

Loan to Value —See **LTV.**

Lock/Lock In—Most lenders can **Lock In** the **Rate** they'll be offering you on **Adjustables** when you turn in your **Application.** They may even be able to **Lock** with a guarantee that, if **Rates** go down, you'll get the lower **Rate**, but if they go up, you won't have to take the higher **Rate.** With a **Fixed,** however, they wait to **Lock In** the **Rate** until just before **Funding** so that the **Rate** will most closely mirror the market. If **Rates** go up during that time, it can mean you won't qualify for as large a **Loan Amount** as you want, and/or your monthly payments will be higher than you expect.

*Tip: Ask your **Loan Advisor** what the **Maximum Payment Scenario** might be on a higher **Lock In**. Also, find out ahead of time how many days it will take for the lender to give you a **Lock In** after receiving your completed loan package. Some lenders will **Lock In** a **Fixed Rate** in advance of closing for a **Fee**. The **Fee** goes up the further in advance the **Lock** is given.*

London Interbank Offer Rate—See **LIBOR.**

Low-Doc/No-Doc Loan Programs—When mortgage money is readily available, lenders offer **Low-Doc** and **No-Doc Loans,** which require fewer verifications of income and no tax returns for self-employed and commissioned people. Although they cut your hassle factor (see **Documentation**), they are usually only available as **Adjustables** with higher **Rates.**

 *Trap: On these **Loan Programs**, lenders often require borrower sign off on documents that not only give the lender the right to get copies of your tax returns from the IRS, but also give the lender the right to give a copy of your **Application** to the IRS. The idea is to keep you honest on your **Loan Application**, but the IRS often automatically starts an audit when it receives one of these documents from your lender.*

Low Income Homebuyer Programs—Government **Programs**, both national and local, to help you buy a home. These range from special **Tax Credits** to outright grants.
　　See also **MCC Tax Credits, Neighborhood Advantage Loans,** and **VA.**

 *Tip: Take a look at the Fannie Mae Homepath web site at www.homepath.com or call 800 732-6643 for an overview of **Programs** and telephone numbers of local assistance counselors.*

LTV (Loan to Value)—The amount of the Purchase Price that can be financed with a loan. On a $100,000 **Purchase Price,** an 80% **LTV First** would cover $80,000 of the cost. In aggressive markets, some lenders (particularly lenders offering **Home Equity Seconds**) will do loans totaling more than the value of the home, i.e., 110% to 125% **LTV.**
　　See also **Downpayment, Equity,** and **Ratio.**

Margin—The amount over the **Index** that the bank adds to determine your actual (or **"Fully Indexed"**) **Interest Rate**

with **Adjustable Loans.** If you have a **Teaser Initial Rate** or a **Negative Amortization Loan,** the **Margin** will be a big factor in the size of future payments. If you have a **Fixed** or some **No Neg Adjustables,** the **Margin** impact will be obvious from the start, because the first payments will be **"Fully Indexed."**

Market Value—The lender's best insurance that your loan is going to be paid back is the security of a property that is worth more than the loan. The **Appraisal** of **Market Value,** therefore, becomes crucial to your getting the **Loan Amount** you want.

To determine this **Value,** appraisers look at four to six other **"Comparable"** properties—homes in the same neighborhood of about the same age and size, which have sold in the last six months. They evaluate your prospective home against the others, weighing things like a better location on a corner, a bigger swimming pool, and/or better condition, to come up with the **"Comparable Value"** of your place.

Appraisers also check how much your home would cost to rebuild and how much it would rent for, although these methods of **Appraisal** are not nearly as important with homes as they are with investment real estate. Finally, they evaluate all their findings together to come up with their **Appraisal** of **Market Value.**

See also **Appraisal** and **Comparables/Comps.**

Tip: It's a good idea for the seller or the seller's real estate agent to walk through the house with the appraiser, pointing out features and sharing a copy of the neighborhood Comparable home sales that the real estate agent used when helping set the asking price of the property. The appraiser will still look up all Comps, and will notice if the real estate agent has forgotten some with lower sales prices, but he or she will be happy to listen to the agent's reasons for setting the price, and weigh the positive aspects of the property into the final Appraisal evaluation.

Maximum Payment Scenario—Spelled out in the **Max Payment** section of the **Loan Evaluation Checklist** in the **Appendix.** This formula should itemize the most your **Adjustable Rate** payments can go up in each of the first five years (the period when it's most likely to be difficult for a borrower to make payments). The concept is based on the possibility that high inflation could hit again, therefore your **Rates** get as bad as they can, then stay there. **Loan Advisors** don't like to make these calculations for you. They'll explain that it's unlikely we'll have double digit inflation for an entire five-year period.

 Tip: They're probably right, but insist on a five-year Maximum Payment Scenario, anyway, because: 1. It prepares you for the worst. 2. The Maximum Payment Scenario gives you solid numbers for comparing Loan Programs. If a Loan Advisor only gives you what he or she feels is a "Most Likely Scenario," you get inaccurate variables from one Loan Program to the next. Federal law now guarantees you should have Maximum Payment and "Worst Case Scenario" estimates, so keep insisting, even if your Loan Advisor tries to avoid the issue.

MCC Tax Credits—A good (but somewhat complicated) route to getting the government to help with your homebuying. These **Credits** are deducted directly from the "taxes owed" line on your 1040, and can mean the difference between your qualifying for the **Loan Amount** you need, and having to wait years to buy your home.

To qualify, your income has to be at average or below for your area, your area must be participating in the program (not all local governments do), and you must go to a lender that offers these loans.

 Tip: The first step in finding out all these local guidelines is usually your local Housing Authority, or call Fannie Mae at 800 732-6643 (or visit their Homepath web site at www.homepath.com) for local authority telephone numbers and an overview of this and other government homebuying aids.

Minimum Payment—Negative Amortization loans typically give you three options on your monthly payment—**Fully Amortized, Interest Only,** and **Minimum Payment.** The **Minimum** is determined by your loan's **Payment Cap** and **Payment Floor,** and usually fluctuates less than 1% annually.

Mortgage Broker—A **Loan Advisor** who is paid commissions to represent **Loan Programs** from numerous lenders all over the country. It used to be that **Mortgage Brokers** were easy to spot, because the name of the company included the word, "**Mortgage.**" As more and more banks and savings and loans merge, more and more of their inhouse **Loan Advisors** have been put on commission selling both their own **Portfolio Loan Programs** *and* **Programs** from other lenders.

Mortgage Brokers sometimes have bonuses tied to selling high **Rate** loans and may be reluctant to discuss the hazards of their **Loan Programs,** but the best ones--like all good salespeople--are wizards at finding the perfect **Program** for your needs.

See also **Loan Advisor** and **Portfolio.**

Mortgage Calculator / Evaluator—Numerous companies have developed software to help you calculate your mortgage payments and costs. The popular home finance programs, Quicken and Microsoft Money both have **Mortgage Calculators** built-in as one of their features. Other companies have gone one step further, and offer **Evaluator** software that not only gives costs, but suggestions for **Borrower Qualification, Loan to Value,** renting vs. owning formulas, etc.

See the **National Money$ource Directory** for descriptions and ratings of these programs.

Mortgage, First—See **First Mortgage.**

Mortgage Life Insurance—Insurance companies often contact you to urge that you take out a special life insurance policy to provide a **Payoff** of the mortgage in the event of a household wage earner's death.

If this is a good idea for you, check with your regular life insurance agent before signing up. Even though your lender may recommend them, usually the firms catering to the mortgage insurance market have extraordinarily high premiums, and we've heard complaints about policies for two wage earner families only paying if both spouses die.

Don't confuse this insurance with the **Private Mortgage Insurance (PMI)** required by lenders on some high **LTV Loans**. **PMI** only protects the lender.

Mortgage, Second—See **Second Mortgage.**

Negative Amortization Loan—These loans have numerous names, including "Monthly **Adjustable** and **Neg Am.** Typically, these loans come with **Payment Caps** less than 1%, a big selling factor over standard **Adjustables,** where **Payment Caps** are typically either 1% each six months, or 2% each year.

The true **Interest Rate** on this loan fluctuates each month, wherever the market goes. When your **Fully Amortized Payment** increases more than your **Payment Cap,** the lender keeps the *required* **Minimum Payment** low and "tacks the remainder back into the **Loan Principal.**" These loans are called **Neg Am** because the **Principal** keeps growing as long as your payments don't cover the entire amount required by that month's interest.

*Trap: We do not recommend **Neg Am Loans,** but we've ended up taking them sometimes when nothing else was affordable. Lower monthlies are great on the budget, but the remainder they're "tacking back into the **Principal"** can add up quickly, sometimes to more than what you originally paid for your home. Two other particularly distasteful **Negative Am** clauses:*

*1. The low **Payment Cap** means that when rates fall, your **Payment Stepdown** is slower than with a standard **Adjustable**.*
*2. Many have a **Recasting** clause, which can trigger occasional **Payment Stepups** ungoverned by any **Cap**.*

*Trap: **Loan Advisors** often downplay **Neg Am** problems by saying that you have the "option" to make the **Fully Amortized** payments—the lender is simply willing to let you pay less if you want to.*
*Since **Fully Amortized Neg Am** loan payments can fluctuate wildly, your "option" to pay is negligible. These **Programs** should come with a heart attack monitor.*

*Tip: Many **Neg Am Loans** come with a third payment option—making an **Interest Only** payment. Most have restrictions that only allow an **Interest Only** payment if it is larger than the "**Minimum**" payment, but try to stretch your budget to do it. This option will keep you from sliding backwards with the "tacked back" **Principal**, where you end up paying **Interest** on **Interest**.*

*Tip: When doing your initial evaluation on **Neg Am Loans**, always fill in the **Max Payment** section on your **Loan Evaluation Checklist** with the **Fully Amortized Payment** based either on at least a 3% rise in your **Rate**, or your **Lifetime Cap**. Do this for each of the next five years. This estimate will be gloomy, perhaps unrealistically gloomy, but at least you'll be prepared for anything.*

Neighborhood Advantage Loans—In order to encourage homeownership in specific areas (usually city center), the government has teamed up with some lenders to offer low **Rate**, high **LTV Loans** to borrowers. Usually there are maximum income guidelines, as well as **Neighborhood** specifics.

Tip: The first step in ferreting out these loans is usually your local Housing Authority, or call Fannie Mae at 800 732-6643 (or visit their Homepath web site at www.homepath.com) for local authority telephone numbers and an overview of this and other government homebuying aids.

No-Doc Loan—See **Low-Doc/No-Doc Loans.**

Non-Conforming Loan—See **Conforming Loan.**

No Neg Loans—**Adjustable Loans** with no **Negative Amortization** provisions. The **Loan Amount** can therefore never grow for any reason. Typically, the **Payment Caps** are higher than the **Neg Am Loans,** i.e., 1% per each six months or 2% per year. However, since **Fully Amortized Payment** on a **Neg Am** can fluctuate as much as 12%, you'll end up paying far less with a **No Neg.**

Online Applications/Searches/Etc.—A great new tool for your savvy loanhunt. Browsing the Internet for information, **Loan Calculators, Evaluator** tools, and **Rates** can save time and money. Many sites even provide **"Rate Watch"** email notices to let you know when **Rates** are moving down— great if you want to **Refinance.** We evaluate the major sites plus give 800 numbers, when available, in the **National Money$ource Directory** in the **Appendix.**

Most lenders with web pages have **Online Application** forms that you can use to start their **Processing.**

These **Applications** vary greatly in their effectiveness. Some lenders use them only to get basic information about you and then have a **Loan Advisor** contact you to recommend a **Loan Program** and finish taking the **Application.**

Others let you do everything from entering the complete **Application,** to selecting a **Loan Program** from an **Online** description, to assembling all your **Documentation** from a computerized punchlist.

See also **Application** and **CLO.**

 *Tip: Browse through the **National Money$ource Directory** in the **Appendix**, and pick several lenders and **Mortgage Brokers** to view their web page **Applications** and instructions. While you're evaluating their **Loan Programs,** take time to decide what kind of interaction you prefer—human or computer.*

Origination—Lenders break up the entire loan process into three separate phases—**Origination, Financing,** and **Servicing.**

Origination includes: advertising, promotions, and other activity to find the borrower; convincing the borrower to select a specific **Loan Program;** taking the **Application;** working with the borrower to assemble the **Documentation** for **Processing;** helping the borrower to refocus the **Application** and/or select a new **Loan Program,** if a **Credit Report** or **Appraisal** doesn't come out as anticipated; and reviewing and **Underwriting** all the **Documentation** to be certain that they conform with the requirements of the final **Loan Program** selected.

Typically, the **Originating** lender is paid for their work with an upfront commission plus some **Fees,** i.e., the **Origination Points** plus the **Closing Costs,** which are paid directly to the lender. See also **Financing, Servicing,** and **Loan Advisor.**

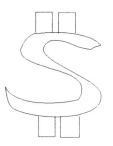

Origination Fee—Also called **Points,** the **Discount Fee,** or, simply, the "**Fee.**" At one time, this was only one **Fee** charged by the **Mortgage Broker** and/or the lender for the service of **Originating,** contacting, and selling you the loan. Today, some lenders charge **Fees** under all three names, and go on to add other **Fees** for **Processing,** reviewing, and **Underwriting** your **Loan Application.**

Each one of these **Fees** for a standard home loan usually runs between one-half and two **Points**—1/2% to 2% of the total **Loan Amount.** As these **Fees** are charged as part of your **Closing Costs,** they increase the amount of cash you need to do the **Close.**

*Tips and Traps: If you're willing to make the higher monthly **Loan Payment**, you can usually **Buyup** your **Fees** to **Zero**. Other lenders will add the **Fees** into the **Loan Amount** so you can cut your upfront cash requirements. Obviously, this also adds to the amount you pay in **Interest** and repay in **Principal**.*

*Tip: When money is readily available, lenders advertise **Zero Point Loans**. When money is tight, or you or your property have difficulty fitting into the **Conforming** and/or **Conventional Loan** guidelines, **Points** can increase dramatically. **Mortgage Brokers,** too, sometimes add their own **Points** to your **Origination Fee**, but not always.*

*Scoping out the current market in **Fees** is a crucial part of your initial loanhunt. Since a several **Point** spread in **Fees** can save you hundreds (sometimes thousands) of dollars, always ask about **Origination Fees** when doing your basic **Loan Evaluation Checklist**.*

Paydown—See **Principal Paydown Payment**.

Payment Cap—Also called the **"Periodic Cap"** or **"Stepup Cap."** The most your **Payment** can go up from one month to the next. Typically, this will be 1% to 2% for a **No Neg** and less than 1% for a **Neg**.

Again, ask your **Loan Advisor** to give you your **Maximum Payment Scenario**.

*Trap: Watch out for loans that have **Recasting** provisions. **Recasting** typically only happens occasionally— say every five years—but a **Recasting** clause means the lender can raise your payments without adhering to your **Payment Cap**. **Recasting** can happen with any **Adjustable Loan**, but is most likely with **Negative Amortization Loans**.*

Payment Floor—Also called a **"Stepdown Payment."** The largest amount your **Adjustable Loan Payment** can go down according to your **Loan Payment Schedule**. This **Stepdown** percentage is usually the same amount as the **Payment Ceiling,** and runs 1% to 2% on **Adjustables** and less than 1% on a **Neg Am.** The small **Stepdown** on **Neg Am Loans,** is the reason their payments go down slower than other **Adjustables,** and yet another reason to avoid these **Loan Programs.**

Payoff—Often simply means the moment in time when the old loan is paid off, however can also mean the **Payoff** statement (or the **Demand** or **Beneficiary** statement) from the previous lender. This gives an accounting of exactly what the lender expects to be paid as of a certain date to close your account. It must be **Demanded** by your **Closing** people in advance, so that the exact **Amortization** is correct and the previous lender closes your account properly.

Trap: Unfortunately, although lenders can usually pull such statements from their computers within a couple of minutes, more and more of them are currently adding a Payoff Fee of more than $50 to your Closing Costs.

Trap: As lenders have reinstituted Prepay Penalties, some sellers and Refinancers are receiving nasty Payoff bills. Be sure you check over all your existing loan Terms prior to making a change.

See **Prepay Penalty** for tips on how to work with this problem.

Periodic Cap—See **Payment Cap.**

PMI (Private Mortgage Insurance)—Extra charges you pay to insure that a portion of your loan will be paid to the lender if you **Default.** Except for **VA** and **FHA** guaranteed loans, **PMI** is usually required on loans of over 80% **Loan to Value.** Expensive. Ask your **Loan Advisor** what percentage **Loan to Value** you must have to avoid paying **PMI.**
See also **Escrow/Impound Account** and **Equity.**

*Tip: If you don't have enough for the required **Down-payment**, you're much better off getting a **Second** from the seller, rather than having to pay **PMI** to an institutional lender.*

*Tip: If you do take a loan that requires **PMI**, keep track of the **Principal Paydowns**. Once you've brought the **Loan Amount** to below 80% of your original **Appraisal**, you can sometimes legally require a lender to stop the **PMI** assessments (clearly a right if your loan has been sold to Fannie Mae or Freddie Mac).*

*You can also request stopping **PMI** assessments when your home's **Market Value** has increased enough to cover the 80% level, but that's harder to achieve and will always require a new **Appraisal**.*

Points—See **Origination Fee** and **Discount Points.**

Portfolio Loans—Loans kept and **Serviced** by the **Origination** lender, and not resold on the **Secondary Market.** Typically done by a small, local bank that knows your market well and can make the loan quickly. Can usually be more flexible on **Borrower Qualifications** and **LTV,** but will charge a slightly higher **Rate.**

Pre-Approval/Pre-Qualification—One of the primary reasons to do your loanhunt prior to looking for a home is to find out the maximum **Loan Amount** you can obtain.

Just researching **Rates,** and then deciding whether or not you can afford the payments, however, is not enough. You need a **Commitment** from the lender on the maximum **Loan Amount** they'll lend you. Then you can decide whether you want to commit to that amount, and from there work out what price range home to look for.

Most lender discussions will include their doing a preliminary **Pre-Qualification** interview with you, where they'll ask your income and debt and verbally tell you that you **Qualify** for a certain amount. (See the **Loan Amount Qualifying Worksheet** in the **Appendix** to find out what that amount is likely to be.)

Pre-Qualification helps in the loanhunting process, but in order minimize the hassle of obtaining the loan after you find your home, you should go the next step to get a written **Pre-Approval** letter stating that the lender commits to lending you a certain amount based on your family's current income and the lender's current **Rate**.

*Tip: **Pre-Approval** sometimes means paying a **Fee**, and always means that the that the lender has to review a complete **Application** with documented proof of your income and expenses. The lender then responds with their **Commitment** in writing. This guards against nasty surprises later, and giving a copy of their **Commitment** letter to a seller, along with your offer to purchase, can give you an advantage over other offers that might be coming in.*

*Trap: Even with a **Pre-Approval** letter, always make your offer contingent upon actually receiving the loan. Rising **Interest Rates** or a low **Appraisal** can nullify the lender's **Commitment**.*

Prepayment Penalty—Also called a "**Prepay.**" A penalty levied if you pay your loan off early by selling or **Refinancing**. Lenders insert these clauses in **Loan Agreements** when **Rates** are stable and occasional dips (plus aggressive loan sales techniques) encourage borrowers to **Refi** and get rid of a Teaser, a higher **Rate**, or replace an **Adjustable** with a **Fixed.**

*Tip: Lenders will sometimes limit the time frame of the **Prepay**, i.e., it will only be levied during the first few years of a loan. When evaluating loans with **Prepays**, always look for those with limited time frames.*

*Tip: Be sure to ask if the home you're buying has a loan with a **Prepay**. If it does, evaluate whether you want to **Assume** the loan, or negotiate with the seller about who will pay the **Penalty**. Be aware that most loans with a **Prepay** are required by law to have an **Assumption** clause.*

Principal Loan Amount—The actual amount owed the lender. Usually paid off each month according to the loan's **Amortization Schedule,** but can actually grow larger with **Negative Amortization** or **Equity Fee Loans.**

Principal Paydown Payments—If you want to speed up your loan **Amortization** so that the **Principal** is paid off more quickly, resulting in your both paying less interest and getting the loan paid off more quickly, you have several options:

1. Loans with a **15-Year** or shorter **Amortization.**
2. **Bi-Weekly Payment Mortgages.**
3. You can add a check for extra **Principal Paydown** as you make a **Loan** payment.

*Tip: We recommend the extra **Principal Paydown** **Payment** because more lenders will accept this **Payment** than will set up short **Amortization** or **Bi-Weekly Schedules,** and—more importantly—the **Paydown** offers you more flexibility. You can add a **Principal Paydown Payment** one month, when—for example, you've just got a bonus—then not make a **Paydown** in a month when you need to pay some other debt.*

*This adding a **Principal Paydown** to your payment, when it's convenient for you, is much less likely to give you serious budget problems than a set **Bi-Weekly** or a **15-Year Amortization Schedule,** but it carries the hazards of any monetary diet plan. It's only as good as your administration ability. If you forget easily or you tend to let things slip over time, you may be better off with a forced short **Amortization Schedule.***

*Trap: The Department of Housing and Urban Affairs reports they have numerous consumer complaints regarding **Principal Paydown Payments.** Lenders either don't acknowledge them, or they set them aside in "**Escrow**" accounts, and only deduct them from the **Princi-***

pal once a year. You're therefore required to continue paying interest on an amount you've already paid back.

*We've seen lenders more willing to credit your monthly **Payment** if you send in two checks a month—one for your regular payment, and one specifically marked for the extra **Principal Paydown**.*

*Check with your **Loan Servicing** office when you decide to make a **Paydown**. They should tell you if they'll accept a **Principal Paydown,** and, if so, how and when you should make it. Be aware that if your **Servicing** company changes, and you start sending your **Loan Payment** to a new address, they may have a new policy regarding **Principal Paydown Payments**.*

Private Mortgage Insurance—See **PMI**.

Processing—One of the functions of the **Originating** lender.

See also **Underwriting/Processing**.

Property Type—One of the basic questions a **Loan Advisor** will ask you is what kind of property type you have, i.e., single family, condo, co-op, 2–4 units, or other.

Many of the best **Rate Loan Programs** only finance owner-occupied single family homes (SFH). Others with preferential **Rates** will do owner-occupied single family and condos, but no 1–4 family. The **FHA/VA** government insurance programs will often cover everything in the one to four family categories, but sometimes they won't cover non-owner occupied (i.e., investment) properties.

*Trap: Properties non-standard for the area are hard to finance. Co-ops are easier in Manhattan, where they're common, but difficult-to-impossible elsewhere. Hundred-year-old Victorians are easy to finance in San Francisco, and difficult in Miami. Farms can only be financed through a few lenders. Review our **National Money$ource Directory** to find lenders specializing in hard-to-finance properties, and always describe your property as carefully and completely as possible during initial interviews.*

Purchase Loan—Lenders prefer making loans at the time a home is purchased, because they feel the **Purchase Price** negotiated between a buyer and seller reflects true **Market Value.** They are always somewhat leery of the **Market Value** appraised in a **Refinance,** because this isn't based on a diligent buyer making sure he or she isn't paying more than **Market** for the property.

Purchase Price—The amount you pay the seller for the home. The **Price** plus some **Closing Costs** and major renovations is the tax basis used in calculating future **Appreciation** and tax liabilities.

Qualified Written Request—Unfortunately lenders sometimes don't disburse the money they take from you for the tax and insurance **Escrow.** They've also been known to miscalculate your **Rate** increases and/or the amount needed for your tax and insurance **Escrow.** The Housing and Urban Development web site (www.hud.gov) lists numerous consumer complaints along these lines.

*Tip: HUD explains that the primary method of complaint is to write a **Qualified Written Request**, detailing the problem, enclosing copies of unpaid tax or insurance bills, and requesting reimbursement or proper payment. Send a copy to HUD, so that if there's a pattern for a specific lender, they can investigate. According to the law, such a request is to have a written response within 60 days.*

Another way to tackle this problem, particularly if you're not sure if you're being overcharged, and, if so, how much, is to contact a service such as the Mortgage Monitor at 800 283-4887 (or see the web site at www.mortgagemonitor.com).

Trap: You may have to pay the tax assessor or insurance company yourself, in order to fend off further action. Then you have to carry on fighting with the lender. Although the lender is required by law to also pay your fines and late fees, consumers often complain that get-

ting reimbursements are difficult. See the www.hud.gov and www.occ.gov web pages for more information.

Qualifying—In order to obtain a loan, you need to **Qualify** your creditworthiness with your **Credit Report,** your ability to make monthly payments with your **Borrower Qualifications,** and the property with the **Appraisal.**

*Tip: If any one of these items don't measure up to the standards required by your **Loan Program**, you have four options:*
*1. Review the **Qualification** in question. Ask the lender to rework it if you find a mistake.*
*2. Shop for another **Loan Program**.*
*3. Change your situation (see **Borrower Qualifications**).*
*4. Change the **Loan Amount** you're requesting.*
*We recommend a combination of all four. Taking a lower **Loan Amount** should be the last resort.*

Rate—See **Interest Rate.**

Rate Adjustment Schedule—See the **Loan Payment Schedule.**

Rate Sheet—Lenders and **Mortgage Brokers** often type up sheets with their current **Rates,** types of **Loan Programs** offered, and information on most of the items listed on the **Loan Evaluation Checklist** in the **Appendix.** Ask for one from each **Loan Advisor** in your initial survey. This will cut down on research time enormously.

Rate, Start—See **Rate.**

Rate, Teaser—See **Teaser.**

Rate Watch Service—Also called a "Mortgage Tracking Service" or a "**Rate** Monitoring Service." An **Online Service** offered by numerous Internet Malls and many individual **Loan Advisors,** who email you regular bulletins about changes in **Rates**. Particularly helpful if you're thinking about **Refinancing**.

Ratio—Several formulas used by lenders to determine how large a **Loan Amount** they will issue. See also **Borrower Qualifications, Loan to Value, and the Loan Amount Qualifying Worksheet in the Appendix.**

Real Estate Settlement Procedures Act—See **RESPA.**

Recasting—On most **Negative Amortization Loans** and some **No Neg Adjustables,** the lender reserves the right to **Recast** the **Loan Payment Schedule,** *without* adhering to the **Payment Cap.** Depending on your **Loan Agreement,** this **Recast** can shorten the **Amortization Schedule** and/or bring the **Interest Rate** up to current market **Interest Rates.**

Depending on your **Loan Agreement,** the **Recast** can be a onetime only event—usually at the end of five years—or be repeated at the end of every five years.

Because the **Recast Schedule** will be determined by market conditions at the time it comes due, lenders usually don't have to **Disclose** it as part of their "Worst Case Scenario" calculations, even though it can cause a horrific jump in your payments.

Record—The information that is officially **Recorded** in the county where the property is located. When the **Purchase** or **Refinance** is **Recorded,** you legally own the new home and are responsible for it and your new mortgage. Often called "going on **Record.**"

Typically, the **Title** with the names of the current owner, is **Recorded,** along with property tax information and details of any **Note** as evidence of any **First** and **Second Loans.** Sometimes other documents, such as mechanics' liens (con-

tractor bills), condominium restrictions, or community requirements are also **Recorded.**
See also **Deed, Title Report,** and **Title.**

Recourse—Personal responsibility for paying a loan. When a lender **Forecloses** against a property, if the resulting sale of the property does not repay the full amount of the loan and the costs of the **Foreclosure** and the loan has a **Recourse** clause, the lender can file for complete restitution from the borrower. Some states have laws against **Recourse** clauses without a more legally complex **Foreclosure.**
See also **Default, Foreclosure,** and **Homestead.**

Redlining—Lenders used to refuse to lend in specific areas which they considered risky. Although they usually justified these decisions with crime and poverty statistics, the truth was often laced with racism. This practice is now illegal, and the government regularly checks lenders' **Origination** records to be sure they are making loans in previously **Redlined** areas. In addition, **Neighborhood Advantage Loans** in those same locations have come to be recognized as good business for lenders as well as borrowers and the community.

 *Tip: If you suspect a lender of **Redlining** or any discriminatory practice, you can complain directly to the OCC. See information in the **National Money$ource Directory.***

Refinance—Replacing an existing mortgage with a new loan. There are four common reasons for **Refinancing:**
1. To pay off a short-term **Balloon Mortgage** (usually a **Seller Second**).
2. To free up home **Equity** dollars for other uses (a **Cash Out Refinance**).
3. To replace an **Adjustable** with a **Fixed Rate.**
4. To obtain a loan with a lower **Rate.**

If you're simply looking for a lower **Adjustable Rate,** there are **Loan Advisors** (almost always **Mortgage Brokers**), who specialize in getting you a **Zero Cost Loan.** The best of these **Advisors** do most of the work assembling your **Documentation,** and save you hassle as well as money. Look for a **Loan Advisor** with a reputation of usually performing according to promises, an **Adjustable** with **Zero Points,** and a **Rate** at least 1% below your existing loan.

See also **Cash Out Refinance.**

Tip: To evaluate the numbers, use the **Refinance Evaluator** in the **Appendix.** Just as important are the loan **Terms.** Try to match or better your **Loan Program,** as well as your **Rate.** Be particularly careful about larger **Lifetime** and **Payment Caps.**

Trap: Never **Refinance** an **Adjustable** or **No Neg Loan** with a **Neg Am.**

Double Trap: No matter how attractive the new **Loan Program** sounds, review the written **Disclosures** very carefully. If you've got a **Teaser Rate** that only lasts a few months, then bounces over your existing **Rate,** your payments over the next two years may not offer any savings.

Triple Trap: Unless you're scheduled to move very soon, never forget you can get stuck with your loan in a tightening money market. If **Rates** soar, there won't be any " **Zero Point Loan** sale" to bail you out.

When should you replace an **Adjustable** with a **Fixed?** If you expect to be in your home at least another five years, look for a **Fixed Rate** at or below your existing **Rate.** If you expect **Rates** to escalate over the next few years, go for a **Fixed** as low as you can find.

When you're considering **Refinancing,** always talk to your existing lender. Often your existing lender has a policy of helping with low **Fee Refinances.** Even if they offer you a much better deal than you currently have, however, you should do a careful loan shop of at least five or six other lenders before zeroing in on the best deal for your current situation.

*A **Refinance** should offer you the luxury of ample hunting time with no pressure to solve **Purchase** problems. Use these advantages to get the best possible loan.*

RESPA (Real Estate Settlement Procedures Act)— The most complete of the **Disclosure** laws and regulations requiring lenders to **Disclose** to the borrower specific costs of the loan under consideration. The law not only requires **Disclosures** at various important stages of your working with the lender, it also gives you the "3-Day Right of Recision" when you finally receive all the actual **Loan Agreements,** with exact amounts due completely spelled out, and you're ready to **Close.**

Unfortunately, although lenders usually comply with the letter of these **Disclosure** laws, they don't always explain the forms well and some loans have been set to **Schedules** that evade the **Disclosures** (see **Negative Am Loans, Recasting,** and **Reverse Mortgages**). Also, it's easy to get lost under the pressure to getting yourself and the property **Qualified** to the point you don't notice a surprisingly large **Fee** or possible jump in the **Loan Payment,** or you don't have time to go out and do more loanhunting when you discover it.

*Tip: Except for some small, local **Portfolio** lenders, you can never negotiate a lender into dropping a specific offending **Fee** or **Rate Schedule** in a loan—you can only select another **Loan Program.** Yet another reason we recommend doing a **Double App** whenever you're working under pressure.*

Reverse Loan—Also called "Home Equity Conversion Mortgages" and "HomeKeeper Loans." If you're over 62 and living in a home with a good deal of built-up **Equity,** you may want or need to use those dollars for other expenses.

Unless you have a large, steady income from outside sources, you won't qualify for a standard **Refinance** or a **Home Equity Second,** because your income won't cover the repayments. Lenders and Congress have therefore devised **Reverse Loans,** which give you money either in a lump sum or in monthly payments, and have no repayment requirements until the home is sold. You have no requirement to sell the home, but upon your death (or the death of both spouses, if the **Reverse Loan** is issued to a married couple), the home must be sold and the loan paid off.

Taking on a **Reverse Loan** obviously affects your heirs, as well as your own ability to decide to sell and move someplace else later. As you investigate **Reverse Mortgages,** think about possible changes in your lifestyle. Consider selling and putting the profits into an annuity that will issue you monthly payments.

Talk with your accountant and relatives about the possibility of selling the home to one or more of your heirs, continuing to live in it and using the resulting dollars to pay them market rent along with your other living expenses. This will allow your heirs to depreciate the property as a verifiable rental property. Or sell the home to them as a second home. They may not get a tax deduction on it, but they don't have to charge you rent. Or borrow the money you need outright from some individual, and **Record** it as a **First** or **Second Loan.**

Compare these alternatives to the **Reverse Mortgage.** As with other loans, there are a number of variations. The items that will define which ones might work for you are:

1. How much money you want—the major national lenders have dollar caps on how much is loaned, no matter what the value of your home.

2. How old you are—the older you are, the larger a percentage of your home **Equity** can be tapped, although the percentage rarely goes over 50%.

3. Whether you want a lump sum, an annual sum, or a monthly annuity.

*Tip: Review the AARP and other **Specialized** web sites in our **National Money$ource Directory**. Also check the mortgage malls for local lenders .*

*Call 800 7-Fannie (800 732-6643) for HomeKeeper information and/or the National Center for Home Equity Conversion (NCHEC) at 800 247-6553 for Home Equity Conversion Mortgage info. NCHEC has a nationwide list of counselors trained to help you analyze various **Reverse Loan** possibilities.*

All **Reverse Mortgage** lenders are required to give you a **Loan Calculation Disclosure,** but the **Equity Fee** charges that allow lenders to accrue **Equity** percentage, as well as **Interest,** is minimized on the **Disclosure** if the **Fee** doesn't occur in the first two years. The larger HomeKeeper Loans, for example, have a 10% of the home's **Market Value** penalty assessed the first day of the *third* year, which specifically avoids **TALC** impact.

Trap: Larger **Loan Amounts** and with a higher **LTV** often mean **Loan Programs** with **Equity Fee** clauses which can cause the **Loan Amount** to grow exponentially over time. The larger HomeSeeker Loans automatically gain 10% of the home's **Market Value** on the first day of the third year. We know of one **Program** that gobbled up 5% of the property **Market Value** each and every year.

Second Mortgage—Also called a "Junior Lien" or a **Subordinate Loan.** On a **Purchase,** this loan is most often extended by the property seller. Typically, payments are **Interest Only** with a **Balloon Payment** of all the **Principal** due within five to seven years.

See also **Equity Second, Seller Carryback, Subordinate Loan** and **Wraparound.**

Tip: Ask if the lender on the **First** will allow you to buy on an "80-10-10" formula whereby the lender provides 80% of the financing, the seller provides a **Second** for 10% of the financing, and the remaining 10% is your **Downpayment.** This is usually the maximum **LTV** you can get without paying **PMI Fees,** although occasionally a lender will allow an "80-15-5," where the **Second** is 15% of the **Purchase Price.**

Trap: Refuse any loan due in less than five years. It's expensive to **Refinance** any more quickly and—if the market goes down—you may not be able to **Refinance** at all.

Secondary Market—Although this concept of bundling large numbers of home mortgages together, and financing them either through stocks or bonds, goes back more than 50 years, it was relatively unused until the 80's.

By that time, three large institutions, the Federal National Mortgage Association (FNMA, nicknamed "Fannie Mae"), the Government National Mortgage Association (GNMA, "Ginnie Mae") and the Federal Home Loan Mortgage Association (FHLMC, "Freddie Mac") had become multi-billion dollar mortgage pools.

Although they were no longer operated by the government, this trio provided two functions that were crucial to the stock market:

1. Some measure of insurance on the loans they bundled

2. A marketplace for lenders to sell loans and get new money to finance new loans

In the 80's, several events conspired to nearly bankrupt the savings and loan industry. First, **Interest Rates** zoomed up into the high teens, and there were fears of 20%+ or even 25%+.

At the same time, a little discussed change by the Financial Accounting Standards Board (FASBD) meant that **Fixed Rate Loans** could no longer be booked as an asset at face value. Instead, they had to be booked at the discount value of their resale on the **Secondary Market**—a problem familiar to bond holders with low **Rate** bonds.

This FASBD change meant that thousands of small savings and loans around the country that had been **Portfolioing** low **Rate** local loans from years past, lost asset value—some losing as much as 50% or 60%.

Meanwhile, the real estate home market went into freefall. Nobody could afford a loan to buy another house. Homes—particularly homes recently evaluated by sloppy appraisers—lost value, and lenders found that even new loans at higher interest **Rates** were in trouble.

Enter **Adjustable Rates.** These loans could be offered at a lower **Start Rate,** and still be booked at almost face value. Enter more stock market participation through "Commercial

Mortgage Backed Securities," which, added to the Fannie, Ginnie, and Freddie behemoths, could finance billions and billions of dollars in loans. Exit most **Portfolio** lenders.

The changes brought down innumerable small S&L's, cost taxpayers billions, and many borrowers lost their homes.

The S&L's that managed to keep their name on the door turned to **Originating** services only. The FASBD bean counters were happy, and major investors, like the Bass brothers, gobbled up huge S&L bargains.

The press sanctimoniously blamed only the sloppy appraisals, and rationalized that the S&L industry had been saved. In truth, the old S&L industry was dead, and a new money making machine had been created. It's called the **Secondary Market,** and it is as vital to the 90's U.S. economy as the cheap, **Fixed** home loan was to the 50's.

Just be happy they haven't been able to sell us the true floating **Rate Loan** with no **Payment** or **Lifetime Caps** that many homes carry in Europe.

Security Deposit—See **Good Faith Deposit.**

Seller Carryback—Also called "Seller Financing." Sellers often help a sale by **Carrying Back** a low-cost **Second.** This is usually preferable to getting a mortgage with high **Loan to Value** that requires you to make **PMI** payments.

See also **Wraparound** and **Second Mortgage.**

*Tip: Some sellers are sophisticated enough to recognize that carrying a mortgage on the home they're selling is one of the safest investments they can make at a decent interest **Rate**. Always insist on at least a five-year **Term**. This negotiation can even blossom into a **First** on a **15-** or **20-Year Amortization Schedule**.*

*Trap: Some lenders frown on **Seller Seconds**. Watch out for **Loan Programs** forbidding them, with nasty clauses warning of **Default** and fraud prosecution.*

Servicing—The lender's management of the loan after it's been issued. With a **Fixed,** unless the borrower **Defaults** in some way, this simply involves receiving, allocating, and recording the monthly **Loan Payment.** With an **Adjustable,** it involves keeping track of the **Adjustments,** notifying the borrower and making sure those payments are properly received, allocated and recorded.

Although most of the interest you pay on your loan is paid to the **Secondary Market** investor that **Financed** your loan, a small part of it pays the institution that does your **Servicing.** Often it's a company set up with **Loan Servicing** as its only business, and it **Services** loans that have been **Originated** all over the country by numerous **Originating** lenders.

Servicing contracts are sometimes sold. The lender should **Disclose** to you on their **TIL** form how likely it is that they will sell their **Servicing,** and the notice of a sale should come from the original lender, not the new company.

*Trap: The Department of Housing and Urban Development has found that loans where the **Servicing** has been sold have a higher rate of miscalculating the **Loan Payment Schedule** changes and/or managing any **Tax** or **Insurance Escrow.***

*Worse, from time to time scam artists set up fake companies, notify borrowers that their **Servicing** has been sold, and they should send their payments to a new address. After collecting payments from thousands of gullible borrowers, they disappear.*

*Tip: Always call your old **Servicing** company at the telephone number on past bills to double check if your **Loan Servicing** has been sold. If it has, pay particular attention to how the **Loan Payment Schedule** and the **Escrow** is managed thereafter.*

Settlement—See **Closing.**

Settlement Costs—See **Closing Costs.**

Settlement Statement—See **Closing Statement.**

Start Rate—See **Initial Rate.**

Stepdown Cap—See **Payment Floor.**

Stepup Cap—See **Payment Cap.**

Subordinate Loan—Also called a "Junior Lien." A **Loan** that is placed on **Title** after the **First.** Typically a **Seller Carryback** on a house, but can be a loan against a site, while the buyer also gets a **Construction Loan.** A seller considering providing this kind of **Loan** needs to check the **Borrower Qualifications** as carefully as an institutional lender will, but most **Seller Carrybacks** are good investments.

Subprime Credit—When mortgage funds are readily available on the **Secondary Market,** lenders sometimes turn to making loans to those borrowers with **Dings.**

The idea is that these "Less-Than-Perfect-Credit" borrowers actually will repay loans... And be willing to pay a higher **Rate** than normal for the privilege of joining the ranks of home borrowers.

Not only do these loans usually have higher **Rates,** they often have other non-recommended terms like **Negative Amortization** and a **Prepay Penalty** (once they've got you, they don't want to let you go).

Like buying stocks from a fast talker on the phone, we don't recommend your taking one of the **Loan Programs** that arrives in your mailbox or lights up your web search. If you need to find money this way, go to one of the nonprofit credit counseling services recommended in our **National Money$ource Directory,** and see what **Programs** they recommend.

See also **"A"–"D" Credit, Credit Rating,** and **B/C Lenders.**

Swing Loan—See **Bridge Loan.**

Take Out Financing—Many **Construction Loans** and **Seller Carrybacks** come due with a large **Principal Amount** still to be paid (i.e., the notorious **Bullet Loan**). At that time, you'll have to get **Take Out Financing**, typically a **Refinance** with a lender offering standard **Fixed** and **Adjustable Loans.**

Try to negotiate your original loan so that you have several months to find your **Take Out Financing,** and a guarantee (usually with a penalty charge) to extend for a certain period. You'll need this if **Rates** are exorbitant at the time the loan comes due, or construction problems come up.

Tax Certification—All lenders require real estate taxes to be paid current prior to the closing a new loan. In some areas, verification that this has been paid is done via a **Tax Certificate** issued either by the tax assessor, the lender or a service company, and there is a **Tax Certification Fee** included in your **Closing Costs.**

Tax Verification Fee—Some lenders require proof that you will continue to pay your real estate taxes in future years. They may require an **Impound Account,** where you pay them $1/12^{th}$ of your annual taxes each month, with your mortgage payment. Another method is to pay a **Tax Verification Fee.**

This is usually to a service that monitors local tax failure-to-pay notices, and reports any defaults to the relevant lender. Some lenders have a department that does this service inhouse. How ever the service is rendered, it will usually turn up as a **Closing Cost.**

Taxes—The "**T**" in the **PITI (Principal, Interest, Taxes,** and **Interest)** payments that lenders allocate to your core expenses when calculating **Borrower Qualifications.** This "**T**" refers only to **Real Estate Taxes,** not anything for the IRS.

Term/Terms—Typically, the "Life" of the loan—the length of time it takes to pay the loan off. Your loan has lesser well-known **Terms,** as well. **Terms** are any clauses defining the loan implementation, such as **Due on Sale** or **Prepay Penalty.**

Teaser—The **Initial Rate** charged on many **Adjustable Loans.** Usually 1% to 3% below the actual ("True" or "Fully Indexed") **Rate.** The **Teaser Rate** typically lasts between three and six months, then your loan will begin adjusting up to the actual **Rate.**

The initial savings in these loans work if you only live in the property three to four years, but it can be an expensive option if you're there longer. Be sure to ask what your **Maximum Payment Scenario** will be—including the **Negative Amortization,** if there is any—after the initial **Teaser** period is over.

Tight Market—Also called a "Credit Crunch." When little money is available in the **Secondary Market** for home mortgages. What money is available is expensive, and often only available via a few **Loan Programs.**

TIL/TALC Disclosures—Acronyms for **"Truth in Lending"** and **"Total Annual Loan Calculation."** These **Good Faith Estimates** are required by law within three days of a lender receiving your **Application** for a **Loan Program.**

These **Disclosures** include federally printed brochures discussing possible charges and "Lender **Affiliated Companies,**" which may be charging you **Fees** at the **Close.** The most important part of these **Disclosures** are the **Good Faith Estimates** of specific costs, although these are only **Estimates** and there is no law that says they can't vary all over the place when you actually get to the **Close.**

We usually expect them to go up, but if they go up more than the market is going up, we seriously consider refusing the loan, and going with your second choice on a **Double App.**

See also **Good Faith Estimate.**

Timing Your Close—Once you've made your deal on your new home and/or your mortgage, and the lender is ready to **Fund,** you have the final say as to the day you actually go on **Record.**

See also **Closing.**

*Tip: Two ways to time your **Closing** for savings:*
*1. Aim for the last week of the month. The lender will insist that you **Prepay** your first prorated **Payment** with your **Closing Costs**. The less you have of the month, the smaller this **Payment.***
*2. Be aware that the lender typically will start charging you interest one day, but you won't go on **Record** or have any use of the money until the following business day. (Lenders don't even clear each others' checks any faster—a suspicious, but legal, practice.)*
*This time overlap between your having to start paying **Interest** and actually having the loan **Funded** is especially distasteful if you're also paying interest on the previous loan at the same time during a **Refinance.***
*Check with your **Closing** person as to whether or not your lender might make arrangements to avoid the overlap. No matter what the situation, however, never schedule a **Close** on a Friday or just before a holiday—you can end up paying several days of double interest.*

Title—The document stating the name of the owners of a property. The name you **Record** as an individual is usually straightforward, unless you want your company or your family trust to have ownership.

Decisions as to "how to take **Title**" become more complex, however, whenever two or more people own property together. The different forms of ownership will have an impact on your taxes and control how your estate is handled. Ask your **Lawyer** and your accountant what is the best way to "take **Title.**"

*Trap: If you do want to own property as a company or a family trust, the lender will often require you to "take **Title**" as an individual before they'll **Record** their loan. You'll then need to **Re-Record** a simple **Deed** transfer back into your family trust, in order to keep your estate planner or tax advisor happy.*

*This task is important. We've known numerous people who have forgotten to **Re-Record** properly, then their heirs have discovered they have to pay thousands of dollars in probate charges, which could have been avoided if the owners had kept their properties in their trust.*

Title Company—See **Escrow/Title Company.**

Title Report—Also known as the "Abstract of **Title**" and "Chain of **Title.**" An abbreviated history of the **Title** of ownership to the property, containing reference to all **Recorded** documents on the property, and stating all current loans or other claims against the ownership.

Needed in order to ensure that the sale is legal and not **Clouded** with claims from someone outside the contract.

Clouds are most often a contractor's claim for payment for work laying a roof, a divorced spouse, etc. Often the bills have actually been paid, but the contractor forgot to remove the lien on **Record.** This means the contractor has to fill in a form to be **Recorded** before you can receive a "clean **Title**" with the sale.

Be sure to review any documents regarding **Title** carefully with your **Lawyer** or **Title** officer, and ask how the **Clouds** can be removed. Some long-forgotten **Title** transfer from a family member who's since died, or a city sewer right of way that may suddenly be activated, can take a long time to remove, and may have a negative effect on the **Market Value** of your home.

Total Annual Loan Calculation—See **TIL/TALC Disclosures.**

Truth in Lending—See **TIL/TALC Disclosures.**

Turnaround Time—Lenders state their **Turnaround Time** in the number of days it takes to **Process** your loan from the day they receive your completed **Application.** Two dates on their timeline are crucial to your planning—their

"**Approval**" or "**Commitment**" date, when they've cleared both you and the **Appraisal,** and they formally write you the specific amount they will lend you (they can sometimes **Lock In** their fixed **Rate** at this point), and the "**Funding** date," which is when you can **Close.**

Some lenders say they can **Close** two weeks from receipt of your package. They might be able to, once in a while, but don't count on it. Usually it takes 30 to 45 days from the day you bring in your completed loan package until the lender is able to **Fund** the loan. Sometimes a **Loan Advisor** mentions things might be "a little slow with a lot of **Appraisals** backed up." Translation: 45 to 60 days to longer. Beware if you must complete your **Purchase** more quickly.

Two-Close Loan—When you're building your home, you need to have a **Construction Loan** to buy the land and do the construction, then you must **Refinance** to repay the **Construction Loan.** This often results in your having to go through a second **Close,** with a new set of **Closing Costs,** i.e., a **Two-Close Loan.**

 *Tip: Look for lenders who do **Construction Loans** and can also arrange the **Refinance** via a **Rollover** of the **Construction Loan** into the standard **30-Year Loan,** without the second **Closing.** These lenders typically charge you less in **Closing Fees,** but the **Rate** may be higher.*

Underwriting Fee—Every time you get a new loan, it seems the list of **Fees** you have to pay gets longer. We were disgusted to see a large, national lender add an **Underwriting Fee** on the purchase of an affordable home that exceeded the **Origination Points** they were already charging. "The loan is so small, we wouldn't make any profit without the **Underwriting Fee,**" we were told.

Underwriting/Processing—Once your **Application** is in, the **Processor** makes sure all the documentation is complete and the **Underwriter** evaluates your living, breathing self and your beautiful prospective home and turns it all into numbers on a piece of paper worth thousands of dollars.

Apparently this term originated several hundred years ago when moneyed folk in England first started evaluating written loan proposals, and wrote their names on a list "Under" the proposal if they agreed to proffer funds.

The **Underwriter** reviews and analyzes all your documents, particularly your **Credit Report,** the **Verification Certificates** or supporting documents, and the **Appraisal,** which have been assembled by the **Processor.** The **Underwriter** makes the ultimate decision as to whether or not to offer you a loan, and if so, how much.

Don't expect to talk to the **Underwriter** or ask direct questions. Your **Loan Advisor** (and sometimes your **Processor**) will relay everything back and forth between you. The **Underwriter** is only interested in evaluating value and risk, not personalities. It's with mixed feelings that we've observed the fairly rapid replacement of this person with **AUS (Automated Underwriting Services.**

Universal Residential Loan Application (URLA)—See **Application.**

VA Loans—These low **Rate, Zero Down** loans are available to more than 29 million Veterans. They used to involve very extensive paperwork, but much of that has been streamlined.

Nevertheless, most **Mortgage Brokers** and lenders either won't do them, or don't understand them. If you want to investigate these programs, look for lenders specifically advertising that they do **VA Loans,** or check the **National Money$ource Directory** for **VA** lenders in both the **Specialized** section and in the mortgage malls

At the moment, the best information we could find was at www.servicentre.com (telephone 650 594-1117). ServiCentre is a **Mortgage Broker** company, which currently only offers mortgages in the San Francisco area, but they are happy to share information on how to qualify, etc., with everyone.

See also **FHA.**

Verification Certificates—Lenders used to require individual **Verifications** of your employment, your sources of **Downpayment,** and any past mortgage payment history.

These blank **Certificates** came with your original **Application,** and you had to send them to your employer, your bank, and your current mortgage holder, 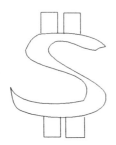 and hope they'd fill them out and return with some degree of speed. Often they didn't, or one got lost somewhere.

Today, many lenders have streamlined their **Processing** on these documents. They rely on copies of paystubs as proof of employment, copies of your bank statements for your sources of **Downpayment,** and **Credit Reports** for mortgage payment history. They still require **Verification** for unusual items, like payment history on a private mortgage, etc., but often you don't have to chase these documents at all.

Wraparound—Also called a "Wrap." This kind of loan is offered by sellers when the loan market is tight, and you want to keep the existing **First** and have the **Seller Carryback** a **Second.** You go ahead and buy the property, *without* formally **Assuming** the **First** (a process often called "taking **Title** subject to the **First**"). Typically, you then make only one mortgage payment a month to the seller, who keeps the portion due him or her on the **Second,** and sends the rest on to the lender as payment for the **First.**

 *Trap: Usually the **First** has a **Due on Sale** clause, which allows the lender to **Foreclose** if they discover this arrangement. They can sometimes do more than foreclose, they can go after you and the seller for damages.*

*Obviously, if the seller doesn't make the payments to the **First** as promised, everybody can get into trouble. The same goes for a situation where you don't make your payments to the seller.*

*We've done these kinds of loans, because they can save significant upfront **Fees,** but a **Wraparound** should only be a short-term arrangement, where the buyer ab-*

*solutely knows a **Refinance** will be possible within six months with either a lower **Rate** or a good **Cash Out** possibility.*

Workout Agreement—See **Forbearance Agreement.**

Zero Point/Cost Loans—When mortgage money is readily available, lenders put **Loan Programs** "on sale," sometimes by offering a lower rate, but more often by offering **Zero Points,** or, better yet, **Zero Cost.** By cutting their upfront **Fees,** they help you cut your **Closing Costs.**

When you look at **Rate Sheets,** particularly ones that were originally designed for internal **Mortgage Broker** use, you'll sometimes see that the lender is quoted as having a negative **Discount Fee.** **Mortgage Brokers** with these **Rate Sheets** may be willing to pass the savings on this **Fee** to you, but not as cash, only as contributions to your **Closing Costs.**

If they keep their **Rates** competitive, this can be a very good deal.

APPENDIX

Contact Lists, Forms and Loan Estimators

national
money$ource
Directory

What follows are 800 telephone numbers and Internet sites for **National Lenders, Mortgage Brokers, Specialized** and **Supplemental Services,** including specialized lenders and government agencies offering subsidies and other assistance.

A list of **Mortgage Evaluator** and **Calculator Software** is also included.

Note that several sites are missing either an 800 number or a web site. Some specific services only work through their 800 number, and with many of the big super sites, you don't need to contact the general web site. Instead, you'll want to contact specific **Mortgage Brokers** from their listings.

This list clicks you into the bigger lenders and the mega malls, but you also need to check out the weekly listings in your local newspaper and what friends and local experts recommend.

The advantage of web institutions is 24-hour **Online** availability, and ease of up-to-the-minute market information gathering. However, their **Loan Program** policy flexibility is still more limited than that of local **Portfolio** lenders.

How you search will make a big difference. If you ask one of the popular browsers for sites having the words "mortgage" or "home loan" in them, you're likely to come up with several million Internet addresses... 99% of which tell you how to get a loan in some other part of the country.

If you limit your search to just your own location, you can miss the bigger national lenders and the financial malls. Many sites don't give you lenders' **Loan Programs** or their current **Rates** and **Fees**. Lenders point out that the loan **Rate** market changes so often, they don't want you calling on last weeks' numbers. They have another agenda—they don't want to be compared on price alone.

Tip: For the second time, we found ourselves spending much more time than we'd expected researching these contacts and web sites, and reviewing and rating them for you.

If you love researching, too, you may want to do some further hunting to check lenders in your particular city or find more exotic Loan Programs than we've listed below. Try a software program like Web Compass that will browse all the major search engines in one go.

Or check out www.askjeeves.com or www.snap.com Online, where there's a meta search service that does much of the same thing, except you can't save your searches or download most information into a file on your disk, which Web Compass allows. If you use MSN, Compuserve, or AOL, be sure to check their Home Forums, too.

Many of the Internet mortgage sites include a **Pre-Qualification** questionnaire. This is the quick way to get a number of customized **Loan Program** descriptions back from lenders. You can fill in a dozen forms in an hour. It beats going from office to office and filling in paper **Applications.**

You are under no obligation to take a loan when you use this loanhunting tool, but be prepared to field the **Loan Advisor's** telephone callbacks.

The lenders' main objective in having you fill in a **Pre-Qualification** questionnaire is for them to make contact with you and get you to borrow from them.

In contrast, your main objective with the questionnaire is to be able to compare several lenders' **Loan Programs** in relation to your specific situation. Doing this **Online** can be much quicker and less stressful than in an ad hoc over-the-phone interview. In most cases, even for the truly Internet empowered, you'll make your final decision on a **Loan Program** after you actually talk with a **Loan Advisor,** and decide that you feel comfortable working with him or her. As we keep stressing, look for someone who keeps promises.

Whether this human contact is on the phone, face to face or via email, have copies of the **Loan Evaluation Forms** from the **Appendix** ready, so your interviews will flow easily, and you'll have the comparable information you need from one conversation to the next.

*Tip: If you know the name of a savings and loan which does many loans in your area, search for their homepage **Online,** where they sometimes have their current **Rates,** and often offer a **Pre-Qualification** questionnaire.*

*Trap: Be aware that your questionnaire responses and/or **Online Application** may not be secure. Think carefully about what information you want floating about the Internet. Do you want outsiders to have access to your credit card, bank account, and/or security access numbers? What about your social security number?*

*Tip: If you come across a **Loan Program** that seems interesting, but you have to give financial secrets upfront before you can get further information, try just leaving fields blank. If that doesn't work, try just filling in 9's or 7's or random numbers. You can always make changes later if you decide you want to pursue the **Loan Program**.*

*Double Tip: Of course, we often carelessly give our financial secrets over the phone to anonymous voices selling our favorite publication or whatever, but mendacious hackers may make the Internet the most likely place for our accounts to get burgled. Many lenders offer browser secure "Certification" with their **Online Application**. Look for it.*

Individual Nationwide Mortgage Source Sites and 800 numbers

The shortlist that follows will hook you up with the biggest national lending institutions. Although the names below are usually thought of as institutional lenders, most of them are actually **Mortgage Brokering** your loan. All of them **Originate** to **Secondary Market** criteria, although occasionally **Portfolio** some of their loans—particularly their **Jumbo Jumbos** for very high income customers.

We don't recommend doing all your loanhunting on the web, because you're likely to miss the small local **Portfolio** lender who is most able to work with any abnormalities in your **Application**. The Internet is a perfect place to start testing the market, however.

We recommend starting out by looking at some of these institution-specific homepages, so that you can get an idea of what's happening with them first. The larger the lender, the more standardized the **Programs** they have to offer. Once you know the market standards, you can tackle the lender malls we've listed further on.

The Steiner rating of $ (low value) to $$$$$ (super value) is based on site ease-of-use, speed, availability of comparable **Rate** information, **Online Application** capabilities, and quality of supplemental services offered. We are *not* rating the lenders nor the **Loan Programs** they offer with this survey.

 Tip: We researched this on a 166 Pentium with a 56K modem. There are bigger muscle machines out there, and some folks have faster transmission, but if we found a site or a software program slow, it was in comparison to the other programs. Judge the ones you want to try accordingly.

Bank of America—$$
This site is currently slow and not very helpful. For information on their nationwide programs, particularly their **Construction Loan,** you're better off calling their 800 number.
www.bankamerica.com
800 219-9147

CalFed/1st Nationwide—$$
These giants have been spending so much time merging, they freely admit they've neglected their web market. They have no **Rate Sheets,** but local contact info is listed **Online.** They've been known in many areas of the country to have good **Loan Programs** and low **Rates,** so they're worth chasing down.
www.calfed.com
800 246-5495

Chase—$$$$$
Offers top-notch daily **Rate** postings. **Loan Programs** are laid out on a grid, so that you can see all of them at a glance, and decide quickly which **Loan Program** fits your budget the best. Set all analysis at "0" points to obtain the best "apples to apples" evaluation. An additional "Total Cost Comparison" calculator grids cumulative costs on different loans for as long a period as you wish (this almost fills in your 5-year **Max Payment Comparison** exactly.)
Gives overview of some **LTV** and other **Loan Program Terms** but not all. Includes **Pre-Qualification** and **Refinance** Evaluators and Calculators. Besides traditional Home loans, Chase currently has loans for hard-to-finance properties like manufactured homes. Our only complaint is that it's difficult to find out how to contact them by phone.
www.chase.com
800 873-6577

Countrywide—$$$
One of the top three **Origination Mortgage Brokers** in the country. Daily **Rate** postings. Only shows "0" point **Rates,**

but **Loan Programs** are not compared side-by-side, so you have to print them out and transfer to our **Loan Evaluator** to see how they stack up. Includes **Pre-Qualification** and **Refinance** Evaluator Calculators.

You can sign up for a **Rate Watch Service,** where they'll email you if you're looking to **Refinance** when **Rates** reach a certain point. Includes **Pre-Qualification** and **Refinance** Evaluators and Calculators.

www.countrywide.com

800 435-6276

Downey Savings—$$

A simple site explaining this medium-sized lender's services, and extolling their ability to process your loan with speed and friendly service. They do **Portfolio** some of their loans, but mostly act as a **Mortgage Broker.** They work with a nationwide network of appraisers and **Title** companies. Their **Rates** are good, but their **Closing Costs** are high.

Inland Mortgage—$$

For such a large and long established **Mortgage Broker** (they did 96,000 loans last year), their Internet presence so far has been surprisingly small. Site includes regular **Rate** postings, but only one **Loan Program,** the basic **30-Year Fixed,** with an 80% **Loan to Value.** Little else, except their 800 number and a nationwide list of contacts. Maybe they'll be developing more as they change their image to their parent company, Irwin Mortgage.

www.inlandmortgage.com

800 984-LEND

Nations Bank—$$$$

Fast, easy-to-use site, with clear **Rate Sheets** and lots of **Loan Programs.** Does not stack up **Fixed** and **Adjustables** on the same **Sheet** or give you a "total cost comparison," however, you can go directly to Transunion **Credit Report,** and order it **Online,** while you're on this site, as well as make an **Online Application.** Offers browser security, and a **Rate Watch Service.**

www.nationsbank.com

800 Nations

Norwest—$$$

Currently the nations' biggest **Mortgage Broker,** Norwest boasts that they **Originate** one in every fifteen home loans made (nearly 200,000 loans last year). Like E-Loan and HomeShark and 95% of the rest of the **Online** lenders, they're acting as **Mortgage Brokers.**

They do not put you directly in touch with the lender that will eventually make your loan, but they occasionally make promises they can't keep, because the lender they're working with changes a policy or **Loan Program.**

Site includes a $300-off coupon for **Online Application,** daily **Rate** postings (without comparable columns), mortgage analysis software, and a good information section on the mortgage process.

www.norwest.com

800 317-3601

Lender Mega Malls, Portals, and Super Sites

These malls have direct links to lenders, and often publish industry-wide information on trends, **Rates,** and borrower tips. Some of them have only a couple of listings in most locations—far worse than the smallest local newspaper real estate section. Others list dozens of lenders and much supplemental information, as well. We review and $ rate them on ease-of-use and speed, extent of lender list spot checked on several locations across the country, ease of cross comparing **Loan Programs,** and inclusion of supplemental services.

America Mortgage Online—$$$$$

This site has been completely revamped this past year, and now has one of the most comprehensive, fast, and easy to use lender malls. **Rate Sheets** for your specific state come up quickly with many choices, each detailing **Rate, Points, Discount Fee,** other **Closing Costs, APR,** monthly payment per $1,000 of the **Loan Amount,** and date the listing was updated. The first column names the lender or **Mortgage Broker,** with a click to their web sites or to email them, and below is their 800 number. The last column has a program that will let you play around with the numbers of a specific **Broker.**

You can call up all their lenders or just a special directory of their many specialists, including VA lenders and **B/C Lenders.**

The only drawbacks are they don't stack **Fixed** and **Adjustables** up on the same sheet, they don't have a total cost column, and their advertisers don't include most of the large national institutions or local **Portfolio** lenders. Otherwise, a search on their site would be enough to give you a complete picture of who is currently offering the best deal for you.

You can order your **Credit Report** and/or a home sales **Comparable** report direct from the site for a small fee. www.amo-mortgage.com

Anancyweb—$

A generalized mall that claims 30,000+ Internet links to web pages, Internet sites, web directories and search engines. International, but very few U.S. lenders, and slow.

www.anancyweb.com

ApprovedBuyer—$$

Unusual concept of carefully pre-vetting a pool of "**A**" borrowers who will then be connected to pre-vetted real estate professionals who specialize in relocation services, and **Loan Advisors** in every state. Claims to help you save up to 1/4% on **Fees** on your next loan and obtain the best **Rates** across the country.

Gives generalized **Rate** postings (which are low), but you can only access actual lender info by giving personal information and agreeing to work with their "approved" professionals. Slow.

www.approvedbuyer.com

888 ABN 7090

Bank One Mortgage—$$

Simple site offering several links to nationwide **Mortgage Brokers** and a description of other services like direct monthly payments from your checking account and **Mortgage Life Insurance**.

www.bankonemortgage.com

800 615-4891

Bank Rate Monitor—$$$$$

A mega mall full of extremely helpful news stories on home and finance trends as well as credit card, checking account, and savings account surveys. A little hard to find their **Rate Sheets** in the midst of this avalanche of information. Look for the simple "Mortgages" button on their left-hand column directory list. Then enter your state, city, and the **Loan Program** you're interested in, and they bring up a truly superior list of both national and local lenders, **Portfolio** lenders, and local **Mortgage Brokers**, with contacts via 800 numbers and/or web site links. Listings include the companies' best **Rates** for the **Loan Program** you chose, plus the **Origination** and **Discount Fee** amounts, etc.

Negatives. Can't stack up several **Loan Programs** on the same sheet. No "total cost" info. Our search brought up dozens of listings for larger cities, but nothing for cities under 300,000. No directory of lenders for **VA, Reverse,** or other specialized **Loan Programs.**

BanxQuote—$$$$$

A finance mall, with info on all kinds of **Credit** services. Their lender list includes Countrywide and other major national **Mortgage Brokers.**

Rate postings stack up comparable lender **Loan Programs,** and *do* include **Fixed** and **Adjustables** on the same sheet. Helpful "benchmark" posting of **Rate** averages for the four geographical sectors of the country.

This site is directly linked to the National Association of Realtors' site at www.realtor.com, so there is a lot of helpful supplemental info. Besides the home and real estate agent listings, check out the easy access to obtaining your **Credit Report** (for a **Fee**).

www.banxquote.com

BestRate—$$

Nationwide listing service for financial services—**Purchase** or **Refinance** home loans, auto loans, credit cards, CD interest **Rates.** No details on **Loan Programs,** except lender telephone numbers. No large nationwide companies or local **Portfolio** lenders. Includes **Pre-Qualification** Calculator. No **Refi** Evaluator or **Rate Watch Service.** Some tips and insights.

www.bestrate.com

Directory of Directories—$

An easy way to get started looking for lender malls. No other lender or mortgage information.

www.dirs.com

E-Loan—$$$$$

Discount **Online Mortgage Broker.** Offers upfront choice between discounted **Online Application** and email/telephone contact with a **Mortgage Broker.**

Nine-item initial questionnaire for either a **Purchase** or a **Refi** presorts which **Loan Programs** you see. This saves time if you already know you want a **No-Doc** or can live with a **Prepay,** but if you want to find out **Rates** on these **Programs** before you decide which one to go for, you have to go back to the beginning and re-do the questionnaire. Since the questionnaire is so short and no identity questions are asked at that stage, this works, ok.

Includes **Pre-Qualification** and **Refinance** Evaluators and Calculators plus **Rate Watch** notification and Loan Monitor services.

www.eloan.com

First Mortgage Network—$$$

A discount **Mortgage Broker** network with several of the basic **Online Services,** including **Mortgage Calculators, Rate Sheets,** homebuying information, and an **Online Application.**

Rate Sheets list a number of different **Loan Programs** on one sheet, but do not give the lender contact information on the listings. They are unique in actually showing some lender's **Discount Points** as a *negative* number. This means that the *lender* will pay whatever is listed as a negative for the **Origination** of this loan. First Mortgage passes this payment from the lender on to you to use towards your **Closing Costs.** The result is often a **Zero Cost Loan.**

www.loanshop.com

Gateway Equity—$

A nationwide network of **Mortgage Brokers** and real estate agents claiming to offer fast **Online Application,** competitive loan interest **Rates,** and mortgage calculation tools. To date, however, their real estate sites are far superior to their lender sites, and their information for mortgage hunters is sparse.

www.geloan.com/servdirs/lenders.html

GetSmart Mortgage Finder—$$$

Easy-to-use mortgage mall that gives you a brief pre-vetting questionnaire to determine which lenders' **Loan Programs** to display. Revises display with new questionnaire responses. Most borrower help resources hidden behind basic questionnaire. Lenders include major national players like Chase and Countrywide.

www.getsmart.com

HomeAdvisor—$$

Microsoft is a relative latecomer to the Internet super site concept, but, typically, they've started up big. Their **HomeAdvisor** site has focused primarily on real estate brokers, but they promise more—many more—lender links soon.

Currently you can apply **Online** and get the latest **Rates** from one or more of their sponsor lenders by email.

www.homeadvisor.com

HomeFair—$$$

Lots of interesting information, including city profiles and a nationwide salary report, but currently short on lender contact info, and their **Rate Sheets** are difficult to understand. Better at real estate agent contact links and property searches.

www.homefair.com

HomeNet—$$$

Has the largest lender directory of the real estate mega malls. Extensive supplemental information on homes for sale and lease, school and education information. Includes several Financial Calculators and a **Pre-Qualification** form. **Rates** are updated regularly, but are only national averages. You must click on the specific company to find out what they're offering.

www.homenet.com

HomeOwners—$$$

Small site that lists only their "best" **Fixed** and **Adjustable Rates,** and focuses on the West Coast, although there's a **Mortgage Broker** network to serve you nationally. Has a streamlined **Online Application** process, which aims to get you **Pre-approved** (not just **Pre-Qualified**) in one business day. Also has a **Rate Watch Service.**

www.homeowners.com

Homes and Land—$$$$

The Internet version of *Homes and Land* magazine, with its well-established reach into communities across the country. Includes local lender info along with its highly publicized real estate lists. Includes listings from E-Loan and Mortgage Tracker, a Mortgage Evaluator, plus a good info library.

www.homes.com

HomeScout—$$

A smallish Internet real estate listings mall, this site has some lender info as well. Includes a cumulative costs Mortgage Calculator, and some national information from HomeShark.

www.homescout.com

HomeShark—$$$$$

Discount **Online Mortgage Broker.** If you prefer voice interaction, call them at 800 HomeShark. This **Mortgage Broker** starts off with a humorous name, and continues with a user-friendly site with explanations about how they **Discount Fees,** exactly what they charge, and a breakdown of other **Fees** charged by each lender they're brokering for.

This low-key approach is reassuring and relaxing. Savvy hunting for **Rates** brought up one of the best comparison chart we've seen on a **Mortgage Broker** site.

They don't, however, stack **Fixed** and **Adjustables** on the same sheet, and they don't have a five-year cumulative expense chart. You have to make up you own from our **Loan Evaluator** form. HomeShark includes a **Pre-Qualification**

and **Refinance** evaluation, **First-Time Homebuyer**/Renter assistance, much background information on lending, and a **Rate Watch Service.**
www.homeshark.com
800-HomeShark

HomeSmart—$$$
Generalized home service mall with E-Loan and several large national lenders as sponsors. **Rate Sheets** are helpful but not comprehensive. The value here is the ability to also check out home insurance plans and compare real estate brokers, as well as shop for a loan.
www.homesmart.com

HomeTeam—$$
A real estate listings mall aimed at people specifically wanting the latest technology in their homes (has Bill Gates seen this one?). Has some lender info and Calculators. Unusual listing of builders and services for "intelligent" homes, i.e., those homes with many built-in electronic features. Several direct links to discount **Online Mortgage Brokers.**
www.hometeam.com

HSH Surveys—$$$
A well established, "insider" research organization that has surveyed more than 2,500 lenders every week for nearly 20 years. HSH indexes their lender **Rate** information on easy-to-read comparison charts. You can view some samples **Online.** To download or order a customized version focused on lenders in your area, send them your **Loan Program** requirements—the cost is between $10 and $20. Information includes hard-to-find data from lenders who will work with owner-builders and East Coast co-op financing. Because the lenders they list don't pay to be included, these are the least biased **Rate** reports on the web.
www.hsh.com
800 873-2837 for lender comparisons and

The Home Mortgage Kit
800 526-4667 for builder questions and
Best Selling Home Plans

The Lending Tree—$$
A smallish, but heavily advertised, lender directory including some of the large national institutions and **Mortgage Brokers,** many of which are East Coast oriented.
www.lendingtree.com

LoanGuide—$$
Extensive information with helpful insights on what various kinds of loans can do for you. Extensive and very helpful, real world **Pre-Qualification** Calculator.
Rate Sheets presented with several **Loan Program** variations at once, so comparisons are possible, although layout is somewhat difficult to follow. Has only a few lender sponsors.
www.loanguide.com

LoanIcons—$$$
A lender mall that puts you directly in touch with **Mortgage Brokers** in various sections of the country by clicking on their icons.
Site checks turned up a fairly large list, including longtime, well-established **Mortgage Brokers,** but no national lenders. Includes helpful links to state government agencies and a useless **Rate** trend guide.
www.loanicons.com

Loans4Less—$
A California only **Mortgage Broker** site offering standard **Loan Programs** plus second home and non-owner occupied investment property loans.
www.loans4less.com

LoanPage—$$$$

A content-rich mall with weekly mortgage trend updates on a wide variety of loans, over 20 ways to search and a 2,000+ database of **Mortgage Brokers** across the country. Their comparison grid gives you their lenders' cheapest **Rates** and **Fees,** but doesn't detail the programs well, so you're not sure how valid the comparisons are. **Pre-Qualification** and **Refi** Calculators, a reference section, and a chat room, where you can exchange experiences with other borrowers.

www.loanpage.com

LoanWeb—$$$

Lender mall with generalized **Rate** and **Loan Program** information, which then puts you through a questionnaire to help you find a **Mortgage Broker** in your area who has the kind of loan you've decided you want.

Although this pre-vetting keeps you from having to deal with a long list of **Brokers** with the wrong programs, it's frustrating to go through the whole process of selecting a **Program,** only to find out it's not offered in your area, so you have to start over.

Otherwise, recommendable links to government help and credit bureaus. You can order your **Credit Report,** or a neighbor home sales **Comparable** report, directly. Mortgage Calculators and information resources also well done.

www.loanweb.com

Mortgage Explorer—$$$

A smallish mortgage monitor service, which will email you when **Rates** have reached your target range. Includes **Pre-Qualification** Calculator and **Refinance** comparison. Lenders are mostly the national behemoths like Citibank and BankAmerica Mortgage.

Unusually large information bank about financing homeowner-builder projects, and listings of builders who will help.

www.homebynet.com

Mortgage Market Information Services (MMIS)— $$$$$

This site offers the best lender selection we've seen, ranging from smaller local **Portfolio** lenders to the national biggies like Norwest and Countrywide. Their information is also published in local newspapers. Site includes a number of good Mortgage Calculators, national average mortgage **Rates,** a daily news section, extensive information, and a chat group.

Rate Sheets don't stack up specific lender **Programs** against each other. For that information you have to go to the individual linked sites, and check out lenders one at a time.

www.interest.com

MortgageMart—$$$$

Very good general background financial information, this site features regularly updated information on all **Rates,** including the national average **Rates** on standard **Loan Programs,** plus the **Rates** on underlying **Indexes** like the T-Bill, **LIBOR,** and **COFI.**

Fortunately, the number and quality of the lenders in their data bank has greatly improved since our last review. Has several Calculators and Evaluators, then you go to lender homepages to find out about their specifics.

www.mortgagemart.com

MortgageNet—$$$

A real estate mega mall. No **Rate Sheets.** Their **Mortgage Broker** list is very similar to the one for the Mortgage Market, but slow to work with, as the page was too graphics-laden for our Pentium I.

Mortgage Payment Calculator helps with **Paydowns,** but not with **Adjustables.** Links to services to repair negative **Credit.** Extensive mortgage help information.

www.mortgage-net.com

The Mortgage Network—$$

A **Mortgage Broker** site that works primarily with corporate relocation programs, providing loans for employees needing to finance the buying and selling of their homes when their company relocates them.

www.themortgagenetwork.com

800 909-6600

MortgageSearch—$

This is more of a mortgage monitor service than a mall. It searches a database of national lenders looking for the mortgage you tell them you want, then emails you when one is found. Useful if you hate loanhunting in general and web surfing in particular. They only search the national companies, however, so probably not the way to find a loan for any irregular situation.

Charge is currently $25 per year, while other sites do it for free. MortgageSearch claims more objectivity because you pay them, rather than the lenders paying to be on a mall.

www.mortgagesearch.com

Mortgages4U—$

A **Mortgage Broker** that turns up on lots of searches, but only serves Massachusetts and New Hampshire.

www.mortgages4u.com

National Mortgage Loan Directory—$$

Mid-sized national site with lenders who can do loans for **VA,** "Less Than Perfect Credit," **Seconds,** and commercial property, as well as the standard **Fixed** and **Adjustable Programs. Rate Sheets** only list generalized **Rates** for your area. They prefer you to fill in their "Request Form," which they'll send to the **Mortgage Brokers** with the kinds of **Loan Programs** that will fit your needs, and then the **Broker** will contact you directly.

www.mortgageloan.com

National Real Estate HyperSite (NREH)—$
Generalized real estate super site that claims to have a national directory and links to agents, builders, mortgage lenders, and other real estate services. The number of lenders in spot-checked areas, however, were few. Little in mortgage information or supplemental service pages.
www.find-home.com

NetCenter—$$
Netscape's home buyer's portal that uses the National Association of Realtor's web site, Realtor.com, for home searching and Quicken Mortgage (see our first national section), for finding home loans. When we visited it, it seemed to have more large national lenders than the actual Quicken site at the same time.
www.netcenter.com

QuickenMortgage—$$$$$
The Quicken homepage offers any financial service a homeowner might want—insurance, investments, IRA's and retirement planning, student loan sources, etc., etc., etc.
Their **Mortgage Brokerage** services are easy to access. Their **Rate** charts stack up several loans against each other, although **Fixed** and **Adjustables** always come out on separate sheets. Does not currently offer special discounts for **Online Applications,** although finds good **Rates.**
Does not reveal the names of lenders, but acts as a **Mortgage Broker** for you. Claims to work with a large number of lenders across the country, and, traditionally, solid company affiliations and product implementation has been a hallmark of the parent company, Intuit.
Site includes various **Rate Watch Services** and mortgage and **Refi** Calculators, which are more sophisticated than those available in the current version of their Quicken personal finance software.
www.quicken.com

Real Estate Databases @ Internets—$$

Over-hyped site claiming "thousands of directly accessible real estate search engines available through Internets' database of databases." Turns up mostly real estate listings or missing sites. No distinct mortgage category nor supplemental mortgage services.

www.internets.com/realest.htm

Town USA Internet Links—$

National area information resource. Most info is real estate, not mortgage, related. Links to several search engines. For people who are investigating a new community as well as new lenders, it includes Chamber of Commerce and state tax listings.

www.town-usa.com

U. S. Mortgage—$$

A national **Mortgage Broker** specializing in fast, **Online Approval** and **Processing.** For employees with a good credit history, they can **Approve** your **Credit** and confirm the maximum **Loan Amount** they'll extend to you in as little as 20 minutes of receipt of your **Online Application.**

Rate Sheets only offer a brief overview of their **Loan Programs,** but the **Rates** and **Fees** seem to be low.

www.usmtg.com

Yahoo!—$$

Over the last couple of years, Yahoo! has been converting itself from a search engine with an annotated directory into a portal/mega mall, where you can search for anything you want.

Their home finance section is only one small corner of this universe, and it brings together Bank Rate Monitor to give you up-to-date **Rate** information, and E-Loan to find mortgages for you. You can visit both of these sites separately at their addresses above, or find them and others as you wander around in Yahoo!

www.yahoo.com

Specialized and Supplemental Services

These listings include lender malls that focus on just one type of loan, as well as national organizations and governmental agencies that can help you with special financing programs.

AARP Reverse Mortgage and other Financial Information—$$$$

The American Association of Retired Persons has extensive information on **Reverse Mortgages,** including Evaluators, past magazine articles, books, and videotapes on the subject. It further explains the not-for-profit National Center for Home Equity Conversion (NCHEC) services. Web site is under construction. See below, **Reverse Mortgages** for specialized lenders.

800 247-6553 for NCHEC

Affordable Mortgages—$$$$

This site has information on loans for low-to-moderate income homebuyers, giving special government programs, **Ratios,** and **Rates.** It also includes some resources on where to find these loans.

www.hud.gov/mortgage.html

Construction Lending Corporation—$$$

One of the few national **Portfolio** lenders specializing in **Construction Loan.** Features excellent consultants who help you find a **Mortgage Broker** in the area where you want to build who can put together financing for you using their **Construction Loan** and someone else's standard **30-Year Fixed** or **Adjustable.** Very flexible about working with other lender's, and therefore can usually offer the most competitive overall financing for a **Construction Loan** package.

1 888 645-6620

no web site at the moment

Consumer Credit Counseling Service—$$$$

This nonprofit organization has offices around the country which can give you specific information on how to go about re-establishing your Credit. Charges for their services are low to nonexistent.

www.credit.org

Call 800 388-2227 for the office nearest you.

Credit Reports—$$

You legally have the right to obtain your Credit Report for free from an agency that's caused you to fail a Credit requirement at any time. Residents of several states can receive annual Credit Reports by law.

To avoid these pesky consumer requests, these companies are rarely listed in your local telephone directory, and only Equifax makes ordering your report via phone relatively easy.

Experian (TRW) discontinued its policy of issuing a free annual Credit Report on request, and now, like the other two, charges (up to $8.50). If you want to pull all three reports, you may be able to get them faster through the Quicken program hookup or two of the credit service sites we've listed and duplicated below.

Equifax (CBI) 800 685-1111 or www.equifax.com

Experian (TRW) 800 682-7654 or 888 397-3742 or
www.experian.com

TransUnion 800 916-8800 or www.transunion.com

www.banxquote.com and www.loanweb.com.

Credit Repair Private Companies—$$

A number of private companies offer help in obtaining your Credit Report, and specifics on rebuilding Credit. They are often not expensive—the ones listed here only charge $10 and $20 to oversee your efforts—but many have earned a bad name for making impossible promises.

Be sure to investigate the Consumer Credit Counseling Service and the Fannie Mae HomePath suggestions before you go to a private counselor. They can help you clear incorrect information, as well as repair your Credit.

Once you've worked on your **Credit Report,** check here for **Low Income** programs and the lender malls for information on **B / C Loan Programs.** When mortgage money is available, you'll find a number of **Programs** tailored for the "credit impaired." They have higher **Rates,** but easy paperwork.

www.badcredit.com

www.imperfectcredit.com

Fannie Mae HomePath—$$$$

This site by Fannie Mae, the huge quasi-government **Secondary Market** institution, has extensive information about how to repair your **Credit** through local programs or how low-income individuals can obtain the best mortgages. Includes a list of counselors in specific areas all across the country, but no longer includes advertising and links to the nations' largest lender homepages.

www.homepath.com

800 732-6643

Flood Insurance Information—$$$

You can reach FEMA (the Federal Emergency Management Agency) to obtain local **Flood Insurance** certificates and **Rates** information at their 800 number below. They have further instructions on how to look up map information on their web site.

www.fema.gov

800 358-9616 or 800 427-2297 x 2297

Mortgage Monitor—$$$

This service from the American Homeowners Association will review your **Loan Payment Schedule** against the proper **Index** and let you know if adjustments have been made correctly. They'll also help you file complaints.

800 Audit-USA

Office of the Comptroller of Currency—$$$
The OCC homepage gives information on how to complain if your lender acts improperly.

Has a complete IRS tax form download and e-file information kit.

Not only is the site easy to access and move from one section to another, it's a relief to find that everything is written clearly and with some humor.

www.occ.treas.gov

Tip: For lender complaints, you can contact them on the site or email to consumer complaint@occ.treas.gov, or call 800 613-6743 or write Customer Assistance Unit, Mail Stop 3-9, 250 E Street SW, Washington, DC 20219.

Reverse Mortgages—$$$$
The two largest **Reverse Mortgage Loan Programs** for seniors wanting to cash in on some of their home equity are HomeKeeper from the giant Fannie Mae organization, and the National Center for Home Equity Conversion (NCHEC), a not-for-profit organization, which has specifically trained counselors around the country to help you evaluate your choices and review pre-vetted lenders. Their information is not currently available on their web sites.

800-7-Fannie (800 732-6643)
800 247-6553 for NCHEC

USAA—$$
An Armed Forces (and extended family) members-only **Mortgage Broker.** In the past, they've offered very competitive **Home Equity Seconds** and national auto and home insurance plans. They've only recently branched into **First Mortgages,** and currently don't have many **Loan Programs.**

Their web site is also not currently very helpful (and limited to members), but they have superb 800-number operators, who make joining and using their services easy.

www.usaa.com
800 531-0340

U.S. Department of Housing and Urban Development Lender Links—$$$

This site has information on loans for low-to-moderate income homebuyers, giving special government **Loan Programs, Ratios,** and **Rates.** It also includes some resources on where to find these loans.

www.hud.gov/mortgage.html

VA Loans

Several of the big lender malls and portals in the previous section have lenders and **Mortgage Brokers** *who offer* **VA Loans.** *Always look for a lender that does lots of VA, because the paperwork requires specially trained people.*

Here are two **Online Brokers,** *who specialize in offering* **VA Loans** *in several areas:*

VA Loans—$$$

This **Mortgage Broker** site only obtains mortgages on the West Coast, currently, but it's got by far the most information we could find on **VA Loans,** how to qualify, etc. with regularly posted **Rates** and explanations of all the **VA Terms.**

www.servicentre.com

No 800-number, local is 650 594-1117

VA Loans—$$$

A relatively simple site for Texcorp Mortgage Bankers, Inc., who aim to help Veterans across the country purchase and **Refinance.**

www.valoans.com

800 411-3768

The Waterfield Group—$$$

The largest national **Portfolio** lender for construction financing. Can do either a **Construction/Perm** loan that allows you to **Rollover** the **Construction Loan** into a standard **30-Year Fixed** or **Adjustable,** or a **Two-Close Construction** and standard **30-Year** for slightly higher **Fees,** but lower **Rates.**

1888 932-5647

no web site at this time

Information and News Services

These sites are helpful for anyone looking for atypical financing, like a **Construction Loan** or a **Reverse Mortgage,** or wanting to have a super current overview of the mortgage industry before going on the loanhunt.

International Real Estate Digest (IRED)—$$$$

Clustered around a core of articles on real estate and lending by the highly respected real estate journalist, Brad Inman, this site has grown to be a huge and up-to-the-minute source of insider information about the state of the industry.

Includes a large lender and real estate mall, with thousands of **Mortgage Brokers,** but little info on their **Programs** or **Rates.**

www.ired.com

Mining Company Financial Services Publications—$$

ABC's of residential mortgage lending and the financial services industry. An insider trade publication information source giving overviews of where to find specific information.

www.financeservices.miningco.com

The Moving Doctors—unrated (blush)

The *How to Talk* authors' site. Information on all items of interest to **Purchasing** or **Refinancing.**

Information on other related books, including *Steiners Complete How to Move Handbook.* Section on mortgage trends and advice is updated regularly.

You can post your personal questions on any aspect of the process for free, and get responses from the Steiners and your fellow borrowers.

www.movedoc.com

National Association of Realtors Homepage—$$$

This site is great for home or Realtor searching, but there is only limited information on current **Rates, Loan Programs,** and/or lenders. For that, you need to go to their linked page, BanxQuote (see above).

www.realtor.com

Mortgage Evaluator and Calculator Software

A large number of Mortgage Evaluator and Calculator software programs have emerged. Now that the perennial best-selling personal finance software programs, Quicken and Money, have jumped into a direct link from your computer to their **Mortgage Broker** arenas, you have an all new ballgame.
Below is a list of some of the best programs, plus some little known ones available from the government. We $ rate them on ease-of-use, ability to handle **Adjustable Loan Amortizations** (rare), and ability to stack up several programs side-by-side (doubly rare, but doubly valuable).

Tip: You may not be able to find some of these programs at your local computer store. A *Savvy Shopper* way to find them, and check out newcomers to the market at the same time, is to shop the *Online* software stores listed below.
These *Online* "stores" often list not only the retail software programs, but also the shareware and freeware programs. FYI—you only pay for shareware programs after you've tried them and decided to keep them. Freeware programs can be downloaded and used for—how amazing—free!

Download.com—$$$
Easy to use and fast. Has a "Shopping Basket" for you to put your software title selections in, before finally deciding whether or not to download.
Their Mortgage Calculator summary list is perfunctory. You have to find the software either on the general personal finance page (which is incomplete) or type the program in by name in their search command. Includes retail software, shareware, and freeware.

ShareWare.Com—$$$
Extensive list of programs that can be downloaded for free, then paid for if you decide you like them. Unfortunately

program descriptions are so brief, it's hard to tell which programs are worth looking at.

ZDNet.com—$$$$

Confusing homepage that is no help on finding Mortgage Calculator software by generic searches. However, if you click on their Software Library icon and then ask the search for Mortgage Evaluators, a good summary list then comes up.

This ZD summary review list is quite helpful, jumps to specific software pages are easy, and their full reviews are insightful. They include retail, shareware, and freeware.

If you have time to browse the site itself, you'll find all kinds of helpful comparison reviews from Ziff Davis publications, like *PC Magazine*, etc., to help you evaluate any software you're looking for.

Now for the software programs, themselves:

APR Calculator—$$

This program has been developed for lenders, and illustrates the number of different methods they have to calculate the **APR**.

Although the program is a free download, and you might want to play around with it to see whether or not your lender is way off base between advertised **APR** and actual **Closing Costs,** it is not a timesaver in evaluating **Loan Programs**.

Their general info and Consumer pages, are very helpful, however, so see the general info section.

www.occ.treas.gov/apr.htm

Electronic Mortgage Hunter Kit—not rated (blush)

Templates for Excel or Lotus. Calculator includes both a "total cost" and a "total interest and fees cost" column. Includes **Amortization** on **Variables.** Does not have a way to stack up several loans on one page on the total **Loan Evaluator,** but does on the **Refinance Evaluator.**

Includes a hyperlink version of our **National Money$earch Directory** to make searches easier. $9.95+$3s/h 415 643-8600

EZ Mortgage Manager—$$$$
Calculates **Amortization** tables for a wide variety of **Loan Programs,** including **Adjustables** and **Bi-Weekly.** Allows entry of variable **Principal Paydowns.** Cost of shareware is $20.

Finance 101—$$
Offers more than 140 different what-if calculations for a wide variety of financial situations, including rent vs. buy scenarios and **Mortgage Amortization.** Includes information on various financial questions. Does a poor job, however, of evaluating **Adjustables** and **Bi-Weekly** or **Principal Paydowns** well. Cost of shareware is $39.

Hi, Finance!—$$$$
Extensive, million + byte program with numerous financial analysis tools, including mortgage analysis that deals with **Adjustables** and **Principal Paydowns,** as well as addressing the influence of inflation. Very sophisticated, but fun approach. Cost of shareware is $59.

HomeBuyer—$$
Good information resource, including extensive contact info regarding **First-Time Homebuyer Programs** in various states. Unfortunately, the mortgage analysis section is not as extensive. Cost of shareware is $12.

Loan and Mortgage—$$$$$
Analyze or track either American or Canadian loans with **Amortization Schedules** for several **Loan Programs** including **Adjustables** and **Bi-Weeklies.** Has the capability to stack up several different analysis on one sheet. Cost of shareware is $19.95.

Loan Chief Lite—$$$$$

Amazingly versatile program compressed into less than 150,000 bytes. Does **Amortization** on the full variety of **Loan Programs**, puts them into a comparison chart, then can be either printed or saved as a file to reopen and re-analyze later. Cost of shareware is $15.

Loan Saver—$$$$

Does **Amortization** on all types of **Loan Programs,** and helps you calculate your **Closing Costs, Origination Costs,** etc.

If you buy it, you get a newsletter with mortgage trend info, as well. Cost of shareware is $30.

Microsoft Money—$$

Microsoft has two "financial planner" programs that are very helpful, a **Mortgage Calculator** and a **Mortgage Evaluator.** Both allow two loans to be stacked up on one screen, and take into account such things as **Discount Fees** and other **Closing Costs.** Unfortunately, it does not allow you to save this information for future comparison to other **Loan Programs,** nor does it allow a printout of anything except a simple, **Fixed Rate Amortization Schedule.** Not as sophisticated or easy-to-use as Quicken.

Basic versions start at under $30 at most software stores and **Online.**

Mortgage Hunter Kit—$$$$

All the Evaluators and Worksheets in the **Appendix,** including the **Loan Qualifier, Loan to Value, Loan Payment,** and **Refinance** Evaluator are ready to load into your Lotus or Excel program. Includes a searchable text file of the **National Money$ource Directory** that can click into your browser for direct access to lender web sites, letters, and forms as well as basic application documents to print out. Cost is $9.95, see back page for ordering information.

Mortgage Payment Calculator 16 or 32 bit—$$$$

The advantage to this freeware product is that it allows you to set up a grid containing numerous **Loan Rates** side by side, and print your results for ultra easy loanhunting comparisons. This also makes a **Refi** comparison easy. Setup and calculations are fast and easy to enter. Mortgage Calculator only, no other bells and whistles. Freeware—No cost.

Mortgage Plus/Tracker—$$$$

Extremely flexible system lets you analyze practically any **Loan Program**, including **Closing Costs.** Allows comparison of only two types of loans side by side on the **Refinance** Calculator. Trial version only allows mortgage amounts of $100,000. Cost of shareware is $39. (Pro version with wordprocessor-ready mortgage docs approved by **FHA** and **VA** is $139.)

Mortgage Wizard Plus—$$$$

Once you turn the **Default** Canadian **Amortization Schedule** into the American monthly version, this program works fine. Can handle a wide variety of **Loan Programs** and **Amortization Schedules.** Only does one analysis to a sheet, but fast and easy to do what-if's. Freeware—No cost.

Partners—$$$

This program is very easy to figure out and lightening fast. Since it's free and comes to you direct from the Federal Reserve Board (at their San Francisco and Minneapolis sites), its supplemental information and insights on how to help yourself **Qualify** for a larger **Loan Amount** are particularly helpful. It has not been updated since 1995, however, so some of the information on grants and subsidiary loans is no longer valid.

It can only do calculations on fixed **Rate** loans. It's somewhat time consuming, but you can recalculate each year on your own, plugging in the **Max Payment** number in order to calculate your "Worst Case Scenario." Can only be found on Federal Reserve Bank sites, try www.frbsf.gov. Freeware—No cost.

Quicken—$$

Most later versions of this popular program have **Mortgage** and **Refinance Evaluators** as part of their Planning functions. These are easy to use and fast. They give you your **Loan Payment** amount and break out the **Principal** and **Interest** on a rudimentary **Amortization Schedule** that can now be switched to a cumulative total mode for analyzing full loan cost, not including **Closing Costs.**

They also don't do calculations on **Adjustables.** You need to re-enter each new year's **Max Payment Interest Rate,** then note the new payment in your **Loan Evaluator** form in our **Appendix.** Cost of economical versions of the program start at $29.95.

Universal Mortgage and Loans—$$$$

Lets you change loan parameters on the analysis screen, so what-if's are easy. Handles all **Loan Programs,** and let's you see what will happen if your do **Principal Paydowns.** Big, 1.5 million byte program, but fast if your machine will take it. Cost of shareware is $14.95.

APPENDIX

loan Evaluation Checklists, Worksheets and Charts

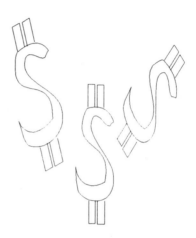

The forms on the following pages will help you organize and clarify your goals as you plan your mortgage hunt.

Photocopy as many of the forms you need so that you can have a fresh set for each lender you investigate. You may wish to enlarge them on the photocopier so that you are not restriced by book publication size.

Evaluation Checklist: Sample Loan

LOAN ADVISOR

Institution/Mortgage Broker	
Name	
Telephone	
Email/Web site	
Licensed/References	

LOAN BASICS

Loan Program Name		
Fixed/Adjustable/Neg Am		
Interest Rate/Mo Payment	%	$
Application/Appraisal Fees	$	$
Origination Fee	%	$
Other Points/Fees	$	$
Total Upfront Lender Fees *	$	
Turnaround—Commit/Fund	# Days	# Days
Sending Rate Sheet		

FOLLOW UP

Downpayment w No PMI	%	$
PMI Monthlly on High LTV	$	
Borrower Qualification Ratios	%	%
Documentation Required		
Amortized Yrs/Baloon Due	# Yrs	# Yrs
Rollover Option/Fee	Y/N	$
Prepay Penalty/Assumable		

ADJUSTABLE

Start Rate		
Teaser or Fully Indexed Rate		
Underlying Index/Margin		
Payment Cap/Floor	%	%
Life Cap/Floor	%	%
Rate Adjustment /Recast	# mo	# yrs

MAX PAYMENT

Total Upfront Lender Fees *	$	
Max1st Yr Mo/AnPayment **	$	$
Max 2nd Yr Mo /AnPayment **	$	$
Max 3rd Yr Mo/AnPayment **	$	$
Max 4th Yr Mo/AnPayment **	$	$
Max 5th Yr Mo/AnPayment **	$	$
Total 5 Yr Expenditures	$	

* Use same Total Upfront Fees
** Base calculations on rates going to their maximum quickly and remaining there. Negative Amortization loan payments to INCLUDE all amounts that could be negatively amortized. © C&S Steiner 1999

Evaluation Checklist: Loan A

LOAN ADVISOR

Institution/Mortgage Broker	
Name	
Telephone	
Email/Web site	
Licensed/References	

LOAN BASICS

Loan Program Name		
Fixed/Adjustable/Neg Am		
Interest Rate/Mo Payment	%	$
Application/Appraisal Fees	$	$
Origination Fee	%	$
Other Points/Fees	$	$
Total Upfront Lender Fees *	$	
Turnaround—Commit/Fund	# Days	# Days
Sending Rate Sheet		

FOLLOW UP

Downpayment w No PMI	%	$
PMI Monthlly on High LTV	$	
Borrower Qualification Ratios	%	%
Documentation Required		
Amortized Yrs/Baloon Due	# Yrs	# Yrs
Rollover Option/Fee	Y/N	$
Prepay Penalty/Assumable		

ADJUSTABLE

Start Rate		
Teaser or Fully Indexed Rate		
Underlying Index/Margin		
Payment Cap/Floor	%	%
Life Cap/Floor	%	%
Rate Adjustment /Recast	# mo	# yrs

MAX PAYMENT

Total Upfront Lender Fees *	$	
Max 1st Yr Mo/AnPayment **	$	$
Max 2nd Yr Mo /AnPayment **	$	$
Max 3rd Yr Mo/AnPayment **	$	$
Max 4th Yr Mo/AnPayment **	$	$
Max 5th Yr Mo/AnPayment **	$	$
Total 5 Yr Expenditures	$	

*Use same Total Upfront Fees
** Base calculations on rates going to their maximum quickly and remaining there. Negative Amortization loan payments to INCLUDE all amounts that could be negatively amortized. © C&S Steiner 1999

Evaluation Checklist: Loan B

LOAN ADVISOR		
Institution/Mortgage Broker		
Name		
Telephone		
Email/Web site		
Licensed/References		

LOAN BASICS		
Loan Program Name		
Fixed/Adjustable/Neg Am		
Interest Rate/Mo Payment	%	$
Application/Appraisal Fees	$	$
Origination Fee	%	$
Other Points/Fees	$	$
Total Upfront Lender Fees *	$	
Turnaround—Commit/Fund	# Days	# Days
Sending Rate Sheet		

FOLLOW UP		
Downpayment w No PMI	%	$
PMI Monthlly on High LTV	$	
Borrower Qualification Ratios	%	%
Documentation Required		
Amortized Yrs/Baloon Due	# Yrs	# Yrs
Rollover Option/Fee	Y/N	$
Prepay Penalty/Assumable		

ADJUSTABLE		
Start Rate		
Teaser or Fully Indexed Rate		
Underlying Index/Margin		
Payment Cap/Floor	%	%
Life Cap/Floor	%	%
Rate Adjustment /Recast	# mo	# yrs

MAX PAYMENT		
Total Upfront Lender Fees *	$	
Max1st Yr Mo/AnPayment **	$	$
Max 2nd Yr Mo /AnPayment **	$	$
Max 3rd Yr Mo/AnPayment **	$	$
Max 4th Yr Mo/AnPayment **	$	$
Max 5th Yr Mo/AnPayment **	$	$
Total 5 Yr Expenditures	$	

*Use same Total Upfront Fees
** Base calculations on rates going to their maximum quickly and remaining there. Negative Amortization loan payments to INCLUDE all amounts that could be negatively amortized. © C&S Steiner 1999

Evaluation Checklist: Loan C

LOAN ADVISOR		
Institution/Mortgage Broker		
Name		
Telephone		
Email/Web site		
Licensed/References		

LOAN BASICS		
Loan Program Name		
Fixed/Adjustable/Neg Am		
Interest Rate/Mo Payment	%	$
Application/Appraisal Fees	$	$
Origination Fee	%	$
Other Points/Fees	$	$
Total Upfront Lender Fees *	$	
Turnaround—Commit/Fund	# Days	# Days
Sending Rate Sheet		

FOLLOW UP		
Downpayment w No PMI	%	$
PMI Monthlly on High LTV	$	
Borrower Qualification Ratios	%	%
Documentation Required		
Amortized Yrs/Baloon Due	# Yrs	# Yrs
Rollover Option/Fee	Y/N	$
Prepay Penalty/Assumable		

ADJUSTABLE		
Start Rate		
Teaser or Fully Indexed Rate		
Underlying Index/Margin		
Payment Cap/Floor	%	%
Life Cap/Floor	%	%
Rate Adjustment /Recast	# mo	# yrs

MAX PAYMENT		
Total Upfront Lender Fees *	$	
Max 1st Yr Mo/AnPayment **	$	$
Max 2nd Yr Mo /AnPayment **	$	$
Max 3rd Yr Mo/AnPayment **	$	$
Max 4th Yr Mo/AnPayment **	$	$
Max 5th Yr Mo/AnPayment **	$	$
Total 5 Yr Expenditures	$	

*Use same Total Upfront Fees
** Base calculations on rates going to their maximum quickly and remaining there. Negative Amortization loan payments to INCLUDE all amounts that could be negatively amortized. © C&S Steiner 1999

Loan Amount Qualifying Worksheet

Lenders use these borrower qualification ratios to determine the size of the annual loan payment you can make, and therefore, how much you qualify to borrow.

They're concerned with the ratio of both your mortgage, taxes, and insurance payments (PITI) to your total annual income and the ratio of all your recurring Family Debt payments to your total annual income.

This Sample Lender sets the "PITI" (Principal, Interest, Taxes and Insurance) ratio at 28% and the borrower's total Family Debt ratio at 36%. These ratios are typical for a 30 yr fixed, but your lender's ratios may be different. Ask your lender what expenses they include in your total family debt.

1. Fill in the blanks on rows g & h in Your Lender's column with the borrower qualification ratios (percentages) that your lender gives you.

2. Fill in the last column with your personal budget dollars.

3. Multiply your Total Annual Income (row f) times your lender ratios to get a dollar maximum amount on rows g & h.

4. Subtract all your annual payments except your "PI" from your Max Family Debt (row h), leaving the amount your lender considers to be your maximum "PI" (Principal and Interest) yearly loan payment on row r.

5. Coordinate your "PI" from row r with the loan rate column on the following Loan Amount Chart to determine your maximum Loan Amount for row s.

Tip: Check this Loan Amount, which takes into account your current income and debts, against your Loan to Value Worksheet to see determine your home's price range.

Loan Amount Qualifying Worksheet

© C&S Steiner 1999

	Catagories	Sample Lender %	Sample Budget	Your Lender %	Your Budget
a	Salary, Borrower #1		$36,800		$
b	Salary, Borrower #2		$33,500		$
c	Self-Employed Income		$5,800		$
d	Investment & Interest Income		$1,000		$
e	Other Income		$0		$
f	TOTAL ANNUAL INCOME (Add a through e)	100%	$77,100	100%	$
g	Max "PIT" (Principal Interest Taxes Insurance allowed (Lender %) x (Your Total Annual Income from row f)	28%	$21,588	%	$
h	Max Family Debt allowed (Lender % x Total Annual Income)	36%	$27,756	%	$
i	Real Estate Taxes (New Home) "T"		$2,633		$
j	Insurance (New Home) "I"		$1,322		$
k	Student Loan Yearly Payment		$2,435		$
l	Auto Loan Yearly Payment		$3,072		$
m	Credit Card Yearly Payment		$243		$
n	Alimony Yearly Payment		$0		$
o	Vacation Home Yearly Mortgage Payment		$0		$
p	Other Recurring Payments Yearly		$551		$
q	Total All Debt Except Principal & Interest (add i thru p)		$10,256		$
r	MAX Qualified "PI" Payment (subtract h minus q)		$17,500		$
s	MAX Loan Amt Allowed at Current Lender Loan Rate	9%	$181,244	%	$

Loan Amount Chart

Find your closest interest rate in the left hand column. Follow that row to your Maximum PI payment column. The intersection is the maximum amount you can borrow with this lender.

Interest Rate	Max PI $10,000	Max PI $12,500	Max PI $15,000	Max PI $17,500	Max PI $20,000	Max PI $22,500	Max PI $25,000
4.00%	$174,551	$218,189	$261,827	$305,464	$349,102	$392,740	$436,378
4.25%	$169,397	$211,747	$254,096	$296,445	$338,795	$381,144	$423,493
4.50%	$164,468	$205,585	$246,701	$287,818	$328,935	$370,052	$411,169
4.75%	$159,750	$199,688	$239,625	$279,563	$319,501	$359,438	$399,376
5.00%	$155,235	$194,043	$232,852	$271,661	$310,469	$349,278	$388,087
5.25%	$150,910	$188,638	$226,366	$264,093	$301,821	$339,549	$377,276
5.50%	$146,768	$183,460	$220,152	$256,844	$293,536	$330,228	$366,920
5.75%	$142,799	$178,498	$214,198	$249,897	$285,597	$321,297	$356,996
6.00%	$138,993	$173,741	$208,490	$243,238	$277,986	$312,734	$347,483
6.25%	$135,344	$169,179	$203,015	$236,851	$270,687	$304,523	$338,359
6.50%	$131,842	$164,803	$197,764	$230,724	$263,685	$296,645	$329,606
6.75%	$128,482	$160,603	$192,723	$224,844	$256,964	$289,085	$321,206
7.00%	$125,256	$156,570	$187,884	$219,199	$250,513	$281,827	$313,141
7.25%	$122,158	$152,698	$183,237	$213,777	$244,316	$274,856	$305,395
7.50%	$119,181	$148,977	$178,772	$208,567	$238,363	$268,158	$297,953
7.75%	$116,320	$145,400	$174,481	$203,561	$232,641	$261,721	$290,801
8.00%	$113,570	$141,962	$170,354	$198,747	$227,139	$255,532	$283,924
8.25%	$110,924	$138,655	$166,386	$194,117	$221,848	$249,579	$277,309
8.50%	$108,378	$135,473	$162,567	$189,662	$216,756	$243,851	$270,945

Interest Rate	Max PI $10,000	Max PI $12,500	Max PI $15,000	Max PI $17,500	Max PI $20,000	Max PI $22,500	Max PI $25,000
8.75%	$105,928	$132,410	$158,891	$185,373	$211,855	$238,337	$264,819
9.00%	$103,568	$129,460	$155,352	$181,244	$207,136	$233,028	$258,921
9.25%	$101,296	$126,619	$151,943	$177,267	$202,591	$227,915	$253,239
9.50%	$99,106	$123,882	$148,658	$173,435	$198,211	$222,988	$247,764
9.75%	$96,995	$121,243	$145,492	$169,741	$193,989	$218,238	$242,486
10.00%	$94,959	$118,699	$142,439	$166,178	$189,918	$213,658	$237,398
10.25%	$92,995	$116,244	$139,493	$162,742	$185,991	$209,240	$232,489
10.50%	$91,101	$113,876	$136,651	$159,426	$182,201	$204,976	$227,752
10.75%	$89,272	$111,589	$133,907	$156,225	$178,543	$200,861	$223,179
11.00%	$87,505	$109,382	$131,258	$153,134	$175,011	$196,887	$218,763
11.25%	$85,799	$107,249	$128,699	$150,148	$171,598	$193,048	$214,498
11.50%	$84,150	$105,188	$126,225	$147,263	$168,301	$189,338	$210,376
11.75%	$82,556	$103,196	$123,835	$144,474	$165,113	$185,752	$206,391
12.00%	$81,015	$101,269	$121,523	$141,777	$162,031	$182,284	$202,538
12.25%	$79,524	$99,405	$119,287	$139,168	$159,049	$178,930	$198,811
12.50%	$78,082	$97,602	$117,123	$136,643	$156,163	$175,684	$195,204
12.75%	$76,685	$95,857	$115,028	$134,199	$153,370	$172,542	$191,713
13.00%	$75,333	$94,166	$113,000	$131,833	$150,666	$169,499	$188,333
13.25%	$74,023	$92,529	$111,035	$129,541	$148,046	$166,552	$185,058
13.50%	$72,754	$90,943	$109,131	$127,320	$145,508	$163,697	$181,885
13.75%	$71,524	$89,405	$107,286	$125,167	$143,048	$160,929	$178,810
14.00%	$70,331	$87,914	$105,497	$123,079	$140,662	$158,245	$175,828

Loan to Value Worksheets

As you start your loan hunt, loan advisors usually ask what you have available for a downpayment, then they quickly calculate your Loan to Value ratio (percentage). This ratio is vital to lenders because the bigger the percentage you put down, the less worried the lender is that you'll repay the loan.

Make the calculations yourself ahead of time, and you'll be able to foresee how your savings fit into your home buying plans. Aim for a loan amount that's 80% or less LTV. You'll avoid PMI fees and get the best loan rates if your ratios are in that range. This conservative strategy means you need to accumulate the 20% down plus another estimated 3% for closing costs.

 Tip: If you're getting the funds from selling your current home, or receiving a large sum of money from any source outside your long established bank account, be prepared to document the source of these funds on your Loan Application.

 Tip: Before you start home shopping in this purchase price range, you need to check the above loan amount against the amount you calculate on the Loan Amount Qualifying Worksheet.

If your income qualifies you for a larger loan amount, and you prefer homes in a higher price range, start talking to lenders who advertise they do loans with less than 20% down or sellers who'll carryback seconds.

If your Loan Qualifying Worksheet only allows a smaller mortgage amount, use that number and look in a lower home price range, hunt for lenders with different ratios and/or look for special programs like Neighborhood Advantage, MCC Tax Credits or VA loans.

Loan To Value Worksheet

Loan to Value Worksheet – 80% Goal Ratio	
Cash Budgeted for Downpayment	$
Cash Needed Percentage – 23% (20% down + 3% Closing Costs)	Divide by .23
Divide Cash Budgeted by Cash Needed % for Resulting Purchase Price	$
Multiply the Purchase Price by 80%	Multiply by .80
Resulting 80% Loan to Value	$
Loan to Value Worksheet – Unknown Ratio	
Purchase Price	$
Cash Available	$
Subtract 3% of the Purchase Price from the Cash Available for Closing Costs Reserves	-$
Cash Remaining for Downpayment	$
Subtract Downpayment from Purchase Price for Resulting Loan Amount	$
Divide Loan Amount by Purchase Price for Loan to Value Ratio	%

Payment Estimator for each $1 of Loan

Interest Rate	30 Yr Monthly Payment	30 Yr Annual Payment	15 Yr Monthly Payment	15 Yr Annual Payment
3.00%	0.00422	0.05059	0.00691	0.08287
3.25%	0.00435	0.05222	0.00703	0.08432
3.50%	0.00449	0.05389	0.00715	0.08579
3.75%	0.00463	0.05557	0.00727	0.08727
4.00%	0.00477	0.05729	0.00740	0.08876
4.25%	0.00492	0.05903	0.00752	0.09027
4.50%	0.00507	0.06080	0.00765	0.09180
4.75%	0.00522	0.06260	0.00778	0.09334
5.00%	0.00537	0.06442	0.00791	0.09490
5.25%	0.00552	0.06626	0.00804	0.09647
5.50%	0.00568	0.06813	0.00817	0.09805
5.75%	0.00584	0.07003	0.00830	0.09965
6.00%	0.00600	0.07195	0.00844	0.10126
6.25%	0.00616	0.07389	0.00857	0.10289
6.50%	0.00632	0.07585	0.00871	0.10453
6.75%	0.00649	0.07783	0.00885	0.10619
7.00%	0.00665	0.07984	0.00899	0.10786
7.25%	0.00682	0.08186	0.00913	0.10954
7.50%	0.00699	0.08391	0.00927	0.11124
7.75%	0.00716	0.08597	0.00941	0.11295
8.00%	0.00734	0.08805	0.00956	0.11468
8.25%	0.00751	0.09015	0.00970	0.11642

© C&S Steiner 1999

To Find Your Total Principal and Interest Payment
1. Find your interest rate in the left hand column.
2. Go across the row to the applicable column.
3. Multiply the factor found times the amount of your loan. *Example: To find out how much your annual loan payment would be for a $175,000 loan, amortized for 30 years, at a 9% interest rate, punch in $175,000 x .09655 = $16,896 annually.*

Payment Estimator for each $1 of Loan

Interest Rate	30 Yr Monthly Payment	30 Yr Annual Payment	15 Yr Monthly Payment	15 Yr Annual Payment
8.50%	0.00769	0.09227	0.00985	0.11817
8.75%	0.00787	0.09440	0.00999	0.11993
9.00%	0.00805	0.09655	0.01014	0.12171
9.25%	0.00823	0.09872	0.01029	0.12350
9.50%	0.00841	0.10090	0.01044	0.12531
9.75%	0.00859	0.10310	0.01059	0.12712
10.00%	0.00878	0.10531	0.01075	0.12895
10.25%	0.00896	0.10753	0.01090	0.13079
10.50%	0.00915	0.10977	0.01105	0.13265
10.75%	0.00933	0.11202	0.01121	0.13451
11.00%	0.00952	0.11428	0.01137	0.13639
11.25%	0.00971	0.11655	0.01152	0.13828
11.50%	0.00990	0.11883	0.01168	0.14018
11.75%	0.01009	0.12113	0.01184	0.14210
12.00%	0.01029	0.12343	0.01200	0.14402
12.25%	0.01048	0.12575	0.01216	0.14596
12.50%	0.01067	0.12807	0.01233	0.14790
12.75%	0.01087	0.13040	0.01249	0.14986
13.00%	0.01106	0.13274	0.01265	0.15183
13.25%	0.01126	0.13509	0.01282	0.15381
13.50%	0.01145	0.13745	0.01298	0.15580
13.75%	0.01165	0.13981	0.01315	0.15780

© C&S Steiner 1999

Note: These factor figures have been rounded off at five decimal places. Your bank's calculation of your total annual loan payment may vary slightly. Some ads and lender's Rate Sheets give you a factor to be used per $1,000 borrowed. The calculation is the same, except you first have to divide your loan amount by $1,000 and then multiply the result by the factor given.

Refinance Evaluator

When you're thinking about refinancing, and want to know what interest rate will be worth the loan paperwork hassle, evaluate the loan programs available on two crucial numbers:

The "months to breakeven." After you've refinanced, this is the number of months it will take for your savings to equal the upfront closing costs.

The "total 5 year savings." We use a five year evaluation because that length of time most nearly matches the average family budgeting timeframe.

You may be planning to stay with this loan the full 30 years. Or you may figure you'll be moving in three. Think about your budget and substitute any number of years on the "Total # Year Savings" line that fits for you.

Tip: Use our Monthly & Annual Loan Payment Estimator in this Appendix to fill in the Refinance Evaluator and see how rates vs. upfront costs stack up.

If you prefer working with software, check out our customized disk of mortgage software (see end pages) or the Online and Software reviews in the National Money$ource Directory in the Appendix. You'll find a number of programs that will run these numbers for you. Note that some programs only give the "months to breakeven" number.

When you decide you're ready to seriously start hunting for a refinance, move from this elementary Refinance Evaluator form to the much more complete Loan Evaluator forms.

Refinance Evaluator

COSTS	CURRENT LOAN	Low Fee Refinance	Low Rate Refinance
Loan Amount	$100,000	$100,000	$100,000
% Interest Rate	8.00%	7.5%	7.0%
Monthly Loan Payment	$740.23	$705.59	$671.55
Annual Loan Payment	$8,882.74	$8,467.12	$8,058.64
Monthly Payment Difference from Current	n/a	$34.63	$68.68
Annual Payment Difference from Current	n/a	$415.62	$824.10
Origination Fee	n/a	0	$1,000
Other Closing Costs	n/a	$500	$500
Total Closing Costs	n/a	$500	$1,500
Months to Breakeven	n/a	14	22
Total 5 Year Savings	n/a	$2,063.66	$4,098.67
Loan Amount			
% Interest Rate			
Monthly Loan Payment			
Annual Loan Payment			
Monthly Payment Difference from Current			
Annual Payment Difference from Current			
Origination Fee			
Other Closing Costs			
Total Closing Costs			
Months to Breakeven			
Total 5 Year Savings			

Personal Credit Report Requests

See **Credit Reports** in the **Supplemental Services** section of the **National Money$ource Directory** for several services that will, for a fee, get the reports for you. To obtain your own, use the written request on the opposite page. Although law requires these agencies to have customer phone access, we were only able to get through to Equifax to order by credit card. TransUnion says they will not take anything but written requests. Although Experian said the web access was only temporarily down and a telephone number was given, it was continuously busy (we tried one time for two solid hours).

It's mandated by federal law that you have the right to a free report if you've been denied credit or employment during the past 60 days due to a report from any of these agencies. You can also receive a free report if you've been a victim of consumer fraud or you're on welfare or out of a job.

All three reporting agencies have the same fees for your **Credit Report.** The fee varies depending on state law where you live. Currently, free reports are available as follows:

One free report each calendar year upon request to everyone in Colorado, Georgia (2 reports), Massachusetts, Maryland, New Jersey, and Vermont.

Several states have small tax levies, but if you don't qualify for the free reports above, you can simply send a check for $9.95 and be sure to be covered.

IMPORTANT—In order to be sure your information is complete and accurate, fill in all the blanks on the sample form, including any Jr.'s, III's, or other generation information, and any other names (after divorce, etc.) that you may have used.

Here are the credit reporting agency addresses:
- √   Equifax Credit Service, PO Box 740249, Atlanta, GA 30374
- √   Experian Consumer Service, PO Box 2104, Allen, TX 75013
- √   TransUnion Corporation—Credit Report Dept., PO Box 390, Springfield, PA 19064-0390

Personal Credit Report Request Form

*Date:*_____

TO Credit Reporting Agency

Dear Sir/Madame:
This is to request my copy of my Credit Report. I have enclosed my check for $9.95 and a copy of my current driver's license or a recent utility bill as proof of my current address.
My full name: _____

Social Sec #: _____
Date of Birth: _____
Mother Maiden Name: _____
Spouse's Name: _____
Employer: _____
Current Address
Street: _____
City/St/Zip: _____
Current Tel Number: _____
Previous Address (within last 5 years)
Street: _____
City/St/Zip: _____
Sincerely,

_____
signature   *date*

Mortgage Credit Certificate

Most of us are aware of how the home mortgage interest deductions taken on Schedule A can be a big help at tax time. What follows is the explanation and the form of a less well known tax break, the **Mortgage Credit Certificate.**

A **Mortgage Credit Certificate** is available for first-time home buyers whose income is generally below the median income for the area where they live. The credit is intended to help lower-income individuals afford home ownership. The tax credit is allowed each year for part of the home mortgage interest they pay.

To be eligible for the credit, you must get a **Mortgage Credit Certificate (MCC)** from your state or local government. Generally, an **MCC** is issued only in connection with a new mortgage for the purchase of your main home.

The **MCC** will show the certificate credit rate you will use to figure your credit. It will also show the certified indebtedness amount on which the interest is eligible for the credit.

 Tip: You must contact the appropriate government agency about getting an MCC before you get a mortgage and buy your home. Contact your state or local housing agency for information about the availability of MCC's in your area.

Claiming the credit. To claim the credit, complete Form 8396 and attach it to your Form 1040. Include the credit in your total for line 47 of Form 1040, and check box b.

Reducing your home mortgage interest deduction. If you itemize your deductions on Schedule A (Form 1040), reduce your home mortgage interest deduction by the amount of the mortgage interest credit.

Selling your home. If you purchase a home after 1990 using an **MCC,** and you sell that home within 9 years, you will have to recapture (repay) a portion of the credit. For additional information, see Publication 523.

Figuring the Credit

Figure your credit on **Form 8396.**

Mortgage not more than certified indebtedness. If your mortgage is equal to (or smaller than) the certified indebtedness amount shown on your **MCC**, enter on line 1 of **Form 8396** all the interest you paid on your mortgage during the year.

Mortgage more than certified indebtedness. If your mortgage is larger than the certified indebtedness amount shown on your **MCC**, you can figure the credit on only part of the interest you paid. To find the amount to enter on line 1, multiply the total interest you paid during the year on your mortgage by the following fraction:

$$\frac{\text{Certified indebtedness amount on your MCC}}{\text{Original amount of your mortgage}}$$

This fraction, which you may change to a percentage, will not change as long as you can take the credit.

Example. Emily's mortgage loan is $50,000. The certified indebtedness amount on her **MCC** is $40,000. She paid $4,000 interest in this year. Emily figures the interest to enter on line 1 of **Form 8396** as follows:

$$\frac{\$40.000}{\$50,000} = 80\%$$

$$\$4,000 \times .80 = \$3,200$$

Emily enters $3,200 on line 1 of Form 8396. In each later year, she will figure her credit using only 80% of the interest she pays for that year.

Limits

Two limits may apply to your credit:

1) A limit based on the credit rate, and
2) A limit based on your tax.

Limit based on credit rate.

If the certificate credit rate is higher than 20%, the credit cannot be more than $2,000.

Limit based on tax.

Your credit (after applying the limit based on the credit rate) cannot be more than your regular tax liability on line 40 of Form 1040 reduced by any credits claimed on lines 41 through 44 of Form 1040.

Dividing the credit

If two or more persons (other than a married couple filing a joint return) hold an interest in the home to which the MCC relates, the credit must be divided based on the interest held by each person.

Example. John and his brother, George, were issued an MCC. They used it to get a mortgage on their main home. John has a 60% ownership interest in the home, and George has a 40% ownership interest in the home. John paid $5,400 mortgage interest this year and George paid $3,600.

The MCC shows a credit rate of 25% and a certified indebtedness amount of $65,000. The loan amount (mortgage) on their home is $60,000. Because the credit rate is more than 20%, the credit is limited to $2,000.

John figures the credit by multiplying the mortgage interest he paid this year ($5,400) by the certificate credit rate (25%) for a total of $1,350.

His credit is limited to $1,200 ($2,000 x 60%).

George figures the credit by multiplying the mortgage interest he paid in this year ($3,600) by the certificate credit rate (25%) for a total of $900. His credit is limited to $800 ($2,000 x 40%).

Carryforward

If your allowable credit is reduced because of the limit based on your tax, you can carry forward the unused portion of the credit to the next 3 years or until used, whichever comes first.

Example. You receive a **Mortgage Credit Certificate** from State X. This year, your tax liability is $1,100, and your mortgage interest credit is $1,700. You claim no other credits. Your unused mortgage interest credit for this year is $600 ($1,700 - $1,100). You can carry forward this amount to the next 3 years.

Credit rate more than 20%.

If you are subject to the $2,000 limit because your certificate credit rate is more than 20%, you cannot carry forward any amount more than $2,000 (or your share of the $2,000 if you must divide the credit).

Example. In the earlier example under *Dividing the Credit,* John and George used the entire $2,000 credit. The excess $150 for John ($1,350 - $1,200) and $100 for George ($900 - $800) cannot be carried forward to future years, despite the tax liabilities for John and George.

Refinancing

If you refinance your original mortgage loan on which you had been given an **MCC**, you must get a new **MCC** to be able to claim the credit on the new loan. And the amount of credit you can claim on the new loan may change. *Table 2* summarizes how to figure your **MCC** credit if you refinance your original mortgage loan.

An issuer may reissue an **MCC** after you refinance your mortgage, but only up to one year after the date of the refinancing. If you did not get a new **MCC,** you may want to contact the state or local housing finance agency that issued your original **MCC** for information about whether you can get a reissued **MCC.**

Year of refinancing.

In the year of refinancing, add the applicable amount of interest paid on the old mortgage and the applicable amount of interest paid on the new mortgage, and enter the total on line 1 of Form 8396.

If your new **MCC** has a credit rate different from the rate on the old **MCC,** you must attach a statement to Form 8396. The statement must show the calculation for lines 1, 2, and 3 for the part of the year when the old **MCC** was in effect. It must show a separate calculation for the part of the year when the new **MCC** was in effect. Combine the amounts of each line

3, enter the total on line 3 of the form, and write "See attached" on the dotted line.

New MCC cannot increase your credit.

The credit that you claim with your new **MCC** cannot be more than the credit that you could have claimed with your old **MCC**.

In most cases, the agency that issues your new **MCC** will make sure that it does not increase your credit. However, if either your old loan or your new loan has a variable (adjustable) interest rate, you wilt need to check this yourself, in that case, you will need to know the amount of the credit you could have claimed using the old **MCC**.

There are two methods for figuring the credit you could have claimed. Under one method, you figure the actual credit that would have been allowed. This means you use the credit rate on the old **MCC** and the interest you would have paid on the old loan.

Tip: As part of your tax records, you should keep your old MCC and the schedule of payments for your old mortgage.

If your old loan was a variable rate mortgage, you can use another method to determine the credit that you could have claimed. Under this method, you figure the credit using a payment schedule of a hypothetical self-amortizing mortgage with level payments projected to the final maturity date of the old mortgage. The interest rate of the hypothetical mortgage is the annual percentage rate (APR) of the new mortgage for purposes of the Federal Truth in Lending Act. The principal of the hypothetical mortgage is the remaining outstanding balance of the certified mortgage indebtedness shown on the old **MCC**.

Tip: You must choose one method and use it consistently beginning with the first tax year for which you claim the credit based on the new MCC.

Where to Deduct Interest and Taxes Paid on Your Home

See the text for information on what expenses are eligible.

IF you are eligible to deduct:
Then report the amount on Schedule A (Form 1040):

√ Real estate taxes - line 6
√ Home mortgage interest and points as reported on
            Form 1098 - line 10
√ Home mortgage interest *not* reported on
            Form 1098-line 11
√ Points *not* reported on Form 1098 - line 12

Effect of Refinancing on Your MCC Credit

IF you get a new (reissued) **MCC** and the amount of your new mortgage is smaller or equal to the certificate indebtedness amount on the new **MCC** then the Interest you claim on Form 8396, line 1, is all the interest paid during the year on your new mortgage.

IF you get a new (reissued) **MCC** and the amount of your new mortgage is larger than the certificate indebtedness on the new **MCC**, then the interest paid during the year on your new mortgage is multiplied by the following fraction:

$$\frac{\text{Certificate indebtedness on your new MCC}}{\text{Original amount of your mortgage}}$$

Note: The credit using the new **MCC** cannot be more than the credit using the old **MCC**. (See **New MCC cannot increase your credit**.)

Mortgage Interest Credit IRS form 8396 for Mortgage Credit Certificates
(see MCC Tax Credits)

Form 8396

Department of the Treasury
Internal Revenue Service (O)

Mortgage Interest Credit

(For Holders of Qualified Mortgage Credit Certificates Issued by State or Local Governmental Units or Agencies.)

▶ Attach to Form 1040.

OMB No. 1545-0930

Attac.
Sequence No. 53

Name(s) shown on Form 1040

Your social security number

Enter the address of your main home to which the qualified mortgage certificate relates if it is different from the address shown on Form 1040.

Part I   Mortgage Interest Credit

1 Interest paid on the certified indebtedness amount. If someone else (other than your spouse if filing jointly) also held an interest in the home, enter only your share of the interest paid. . | 1 |

2 Enter the certificate credit rate shown on your mortgage credit certificate . . . . | 2 | %

3 If line 2 is 20% or less, multiply line 1 by line 2. If line 2 is more than 20%, or if you refinanced your mortgage and received a reissued certificate, see instructions for amount to enter. You must reduce your mortgage interest deduction on Schedule A (Form 1040) by the line 3 amount | 3 |

4 Enter any credit carryforward from 1995 (line 18 of your 1997 Form 8396) . . . . . . | 4 |

5 Enter any credit carryforward from 1996 (line 16 of your 1997 Form 8396) . . . . . . | 5 |

6 Enter any credit carryforward from 1997 (line 19 of your 1997 Form 8396) . . . . . . | 6 |

7 Add lines 3 through 6. . . . . | 7 |

8 Enter the amount from Form 1040, line 40. . . . . | 8 |

9 Add the amounts from Form 1040, lines 41 through 44, and enter the total. . . . . . | 9 |

10 Subtract line 9 from line 8. If zero or less, enter -0-. . . . . | 10 |

11 **Mortgage Interest Credit.** Enter the smaller of line 7 or line 10 here. Also include this amount in the total on Form 1040, line 47. Be sure to check box b on that line . . . . . . | 11 |

Part II   Mortgage Interest Credit Carryforward to 1999. (Complete only if line 11 is less than line 7.)

12 Add lines 3 and 4 . . . . | 12 |

13 Enter the amount from line 7 . . . . | 13 |

14 Enter the larger of line 11 or line 12. . . . . | 14 |

15 Subtract line 14 from line 13 . . . . | 15 |

16 1997 credit carryforward to 1999. Enter the smaller of line 6 or line 15 . . . . . . | 16 |

17 Subtract line 16 from line 15 . . . . | 17 |

18 1996 credit carryforward to 1999. Enter the smaller of line 5 or line 17 . . . . . . | 18 |

19 1998 credit carryforward to 1999. Subtract line 11 from line 3. If zero or less, enter -0-. . | 19 |

General Instructions

Purpose of Form

Use Form 8396 to figure the mortgage interest credit for 1998 and any carryforward to 1999.

Who May Claim the Credit

You may claim the credit only if you were issued a qualified Mortgage Credit Certificate (MCC) by a state or local governmental unit or agency under a qualified mortgage credit certificate program.

For Paperwork Reduction Act Notice, see back of form.

Caution: Certificates issued by the Federal Housing Administration, Department of Veterans Affairs, and Farmers Home Administration, and Homestead Staff Exemption Certificates do not qualify for the credit.

The home to which the certificate relates must be your main home and must also be located in the jurisdiction of the governmental unit that issued the certificate.

If the interest on the mortgage was paid to a related person, you cannot claim the credit.

Cat. No. 62502X   Form 8396 (1998)

Electronic Mortgage Hunter Kit

IBM computer disk packed with the software and contacts you need for all electronic mortgage hunting and analysis.

COMPLETE MORTGAGE HUNT EVALUATION SOFTWARE

Ready-to-run templates plug into your Excel or Lotus programs to give you ultra fast calculations on:

√ **Loan Amount Qualifying Worksheet.** How much loan the bank will say you can afford, with item checklists to be sure you're credited with all your income sources.

√ **Loan to Value Worksheets** to calculate what price home you can buy without paying PMI, plus evaluate a variety of what-if's.

√ **Refinance Evaluator** indicates what interest rate makes refinancing a good idea and compares low rates to low fees.

√ **Loan Payment Calculator** for monthly and annual payments, plus cumulative costs for evaluating adjustables and negative amortization loans.

√ **Loan Evaluation Checklist** includes contact questionnaire plus our unique five year "apples to apples" comparisons. This program will make it easy to evaluate fixed vs. adjustables vs. whatever other loan program you're investigating.

PLUS
COMPLETE NATIONAL MONEY$OURCE DIRECTORY ON DISK

Searchable text file with all the **Money$ource** information and loan sources in html code, ready to load into your web browser for instant click-on links to recommended web pages. The fast and efficient way to do your mortgage hunting.

Email: mortgagedisk@movedoc.com or
IIP, Mortgagedisk, 3357 - 21st Street, San Francisco, CA 94110

ORDER FORM
Electronic Mortgage Hunter Kit

IIP Orders -- Mortgagedisk
3357 - 21st Street
San Francisco, CA 94110

Please rush my timesaving mortgage disk

Mortgage Kit on disk $9.95 (plus $3.00 shipping and handling)

Name:_____(print)

Street:_____(print)

City/St/Zip:_____(print)

Credit Card #:_____

Expiration Date:____/____ Signature:_____

or Check Enclosed ( )

ORDER FORM
Steiners Complete How to Move Handbook

IIP Orders -- MovingHandbook
3357 - 21st Street,
San Francisco, CA 94110

Please rush 374 page handbook

Complete How to Move Handbook $14.95 (plus $3.00 shipping)

Name:_____(print)

Street:_____(print)

City/St/Zip:_____(print)

Credit Card #:_____

Expiration Date:____/____ Signature:_____

or Check Enclosed ( )